VICTORIA TRAVEL GUIDE

2025 Complete Companion To Explore The Garden State In Australia Like A Local With Everything To Know, Travel Hacks, Itineraries & More

Gianna McMillon

Copyright

© Gianna McMillon, 2024.

All rights reserved.

No part of this publication may be reproduced, distributed, or transmitted in any form or by any means, including photocopying, recording, or other electronic or mechanical methods, without the prior written permission of the publisher, except in the case of brief quotations embodied in critical reviews and certain other noncommercial uses permitted by copyright law.

All images, graphics, and content within this guide are either owned by Gianna McMillon or used with permission from their respective owners. Any trademarks, service marks, product names, or named features are assumed to be the property of their respective owners and are used only for reference. There is no implied endorsement if we use one of these terms. Unauthorized use of any content in this publication may violate copyright, trademark, and other laws.

About The Author

Gianna McMillon is an avid traveler and seasoned travel guide author who has spent over two decades exploring the far corners of the world. Born with an insatiable curiosity and a love for adventure, Gianna has transformed her passion for travel into a successful writing career, inspiring countless readers to embark on their own journeys.

Gianna's travel guides are renowned for their meticulous detail, vivid descriptions, and practical advice, making them essential companions for travelers of all kinds. Her expertise spans diverse destinations, from the bustling streets of Tokyo and the romantic boulevards of Paris to the serene landscapes of New Zealand and the exotic locales of Southeast Asia.

With a background in cultural anthropology and a flair for storytelling, Gianna brings a unique perspective to her writing. She delves beyond the typical tourist attractions, uncovering hidden gems and local secrets that offer readers an authentic and immersive experience. Her guides not only provide logistical insights but also enrich the travel experience with historical context, cultural nuances, and personal anecdotes.

Gianna's work has been featured in prominent travel magazines and online platforms, earning her a loyal following of readers who eagerly anticipate her next adventure. When she's not exploring new destinations, Gianna enjoys sharing her experiences through engaging talks and workshops, inspiring others to see the world with fresh eyes.

Whether you're a seasoned traveler or a first-time explorer, Gianna McMillon's travel guides will equip you with the knowledge and inspiration to make your journey unforgettable.

TABLE OF CONTENTS

INTRODUCTION 7
    A Glimpse Of Victoria..............................7
    Why Visit In 2025....................................9
Chapter 2 13
ESSENTIAL PLANNING....................................13
    Best Times To Visit.................................13
    Visa And Travel Requirements...............17
    Packing Tips...22
Chapter 3 27
SPENDING WISELY..27
    Budgeting Your Trip...............................27
    Cost-Saving Tips....................................31
    Best Value For Money Experiences 36
Chapter 4 41
GETTING AROUND 41
    Transportation Options 41
    Driving In Victoria..................................46
    Navigating Public Transit 52
Chapter 5 55
WHERE TO STAY...55
    Accommodation Types 55
    Top Hotels And Hostels..........................58
    Unique Stays 62
Chapter 6 67
FOOD AND DRINK 67

Victoria's Culinary Scene 67
Must-try Local Dishes 71
Wine And Coffee Culture 75
Chapter 7 .... **81**
ADVENTURES AND ACTIVITIES **81**
Outdoor Adventures 81
Art, Culture, And Festivals 86
Family-friendly Activities 91
Chapter 8 .... **97**
STAYING SAFE AND GREEN **97**
Travel Safety Tips 97
Sustainable Tourism In Victoria 101
Chapter 9 .... **107**
SAMPLED ITINERARIES **107**
Iconic Road Trips 107
Weekend Escapes 112
Comprehensive City And Regional Tours .. 118
Chapter 10 .... **126**
NOTABLE SITES AND TOP TOURIST SPOTS 126
Melbourne Highlights 126
Great Ocean Road And Twelve Apostles 131
Phillip Island And Wildlife Parks 134
Yarra Valley And Dandenong Ranges 140
CONCLUSION **146**
Making The Most Of Victoria 146
Final Tips For An Unforgettable Trip 147

INTRODUCTION

A Glimpse Of Victoria

Nestled in the southeastern corner of Australia, Victoria is a state that effortlessly blends natural beauty, vibrant cityscapes, and rich cultural heritage. Though it is the smallest mainland state by area, Victoria punches well above its weight when it comes to offering experiences for every type of traveler. From the bustling streets of Melbourne, its cosmopolitan capital, to the serene coastline of the Great Ocean Road, Victoria captivates with its diverse landscapes, culinary delights, and world-class attractions.

A State of Contrasts

Victoria's appeal lies in its ability to cater to every mood and preference. Fancy a day amidst skyscrapers, street art, and fine dining? Melbourne, often ranked as one of the world's most livable cities, is your destination. Craving a retreat to nature? Head to the Grampians National Park for rugged mountain views or explore the lush greenery of the Dandenong Ranges. Victoria is also home to unique wildlife, like the penguins of Phillip Island and the koalas of Cape Otway.

Cultural and Historical Richness
Victoria has a fascinating cultural story shaped by its indigenous heritage and colonial past. The Wurundjeri, Boonwurrung, and other First Nations peoples have lived in the area for tens of thousands of years, and their enduring connection to the land is celebrated through art, festivals, and cultural centers across the state. Post-European settlement, Victoria's fortunes boomed during the Gold Rush of the 1850s, leaving behind historic towns such as Ballarat and Bendigo, where you can relive the era's opulence.

Climate and Seasons
Victoria enjoys four distinct seasons, making it a year-round destination. Summers are perfect for coastal adventures, autumn showcases vibrant foliage in regions like Bright, winters are cozy in the alpine areas like Mount Buller, and spring bursts with colorful blooms in gardens and parks.

With its boundless charm and a little something for everyone, Victoria sets the stage for a journey you'll never forget.

Why Visit In 2025

Victoria is a destination that continuously reinvents itself, and 2025 is set to be an exceptional year to experience everything this vibrant Australian state has to offer. Whether you're drawn to its cosmopolitan cities, breathtaking landscapes, or rich cultural tapestry, Victoria is stepping into the spotlight with fresh attractions, sustainable tourism initiatives, and unmissable events. Here's why you should make it a top destination in 2025.

A Fresh Take on Classic Destinations
Victoria's iconic attractions are getting exciting updates. The Great Ocean Road, a bucket-list destination, now features enhanced visitor facilities and eco-friendly viewpoints, ensuring sustainable enjoyment of its stunning coastline and the world-famous Twelve Apostles. Meanwhile, Melbourne's vibrant neighborhoods continue to thrive, with new street art installations, culinary pop-ups, and revitalized markets offering unique experiences to visitors.

Major Events and Festivals

In 2025, Victoria will host a series of major events that celebrate its artistic, cultural, and sporting spirit.
- Melbourne Food & Wine Festival: Enjoy innovative cuisine, masterclasses, and wine-tasting experiences.
- AFL Grand Final at the MCG: A must for sports enthusiasts, showcasing Australia's beloved game.
- Melbourne International Arts Festival: Featuring world-class performances in theater, music, and dance.
- Phillip Island Nature Festival: Celebrate wildlife and conservation efforts on this scenic island.

These events highlight the diversity of experiences Victoria offers, making 2025 the perfect year to immerse yourself in its festive atmosphere.

Thriving Eco-Tourism and Sustainability

Victoria is leading the way in sustainable tourism, with initiatives aimed at preserving its natural beauty and promoting eco-friendly travel. From guided tours focusing on indigenous heritage to eco-lodges in regions like the Otway Ranges, travelers can enjoy meaningful experiences while minimizing their environmental footprint. New programs are also being introduced to protect the Great Barrier Reef of the South, the vibrant kelp forests along the coastline.

Accessible and Innovative Infrastructure
Traveling in Victoria is easier than ever, thanks to continued investments in infrastructure. The newly upgraded Melbourne Airport ensures seamless international and domestic connections, while the expansion of regional rail services makes exploring destinations like Bendigo, Ballarat, and Geelong more convenient. Cyclists will also enjoy the newly developed Victorian Rail Trails, perfect for scenic bike rides through the countryside.

A Year of Culinary Excellence
Food lovers are in for a treat in 2025, as Victoria continues to excel in the culinary arts. The Yarra Valley and Mornington Peninsula are celebrating anniversaries of their wine trails with special tours and tasting events, while Melbourne remains a global food capital, offering everything from award-winning fine dining to creative street food. Regional towns like Daylesford are gaining fame for their farm-to-table dining experiences, making Victoria a gastronomic paradise.

Rediscovering Hidden Gems
Beyond the well-trodden paths, Victoria in 2025 offers opportunities to uncover hidden treasures. Explore lesser-known destinations like:

- Wilson's Promontory National Park: An untouched haven for hiking and wildlife spotting.
- Beechworth: A charming historic town with Gold Rush history.
- Macedon Ranges: Known for tranquil gardens and boutique wineries.

A Perfect Time for First-Time and Returning Visitors

Whether you're visiting Victoria for the first time or returning to rediscover its charm, 2025 promises a blend of the familiar and the new. Iconic landmarks remain timeless, but with fresh twists that add excitement for seasoned travelers.

Make Victoria Your Destination in 2025

With its perfect mix of cultural vibrancy, natural beauty, and innovative tourism, Victoria offers endless reasons to visit in 2025. Whether you seek adventure, relaxation, or inspiration, this diverse state is ready to deliver unforgettable experiences. It's time to pack your bags and let Victoria's magic unfold.

Chapter 2

ESSENTIAL PLANNING

Best Times To Visit

Victoria's diverse landscapes and vibrant culture make it a year-round destination, but the best time to visit depends on the experiences you're seeking. From bustling city events to serene natural escapes, each season in Victoria offers something unique. Here's a guide to help you choose the best time to visit based on weather, events, and activities.

Summer (December to February)
Best For: Beach days, outdoor festivals, and coastal drives
Victoria comes alive in the summer with long, sunny days and warm weather, making it the ideal season for outdoor adventures.

- Coastal Attractions: The Great Ocean Road is at its best during summer, with clear skies and calm seas perfect for surfing and beachcombing.
- Festivals Galore: Summer sees major events like the Australian Open in Melbourne and music festivals such as Falls Festival and St. Jerome's Laneway Festival.
- Wine Regions: The Yarra Valley and Mornington Peninsula are perfect for al fresco wine tastings.

Weather: Temperatures range from 25°C to 35°C (77°F to 95°F), but coastal areas often enjoy cooler sea breezes.

Autumn (March to May)
Best For: Scenic drives, food and wine, and cooler outdoor activities
Autumn in Victoria is a stunning season, with crisp air and vibrant foliage painting the countryside in hues of red, orange, and gold.
- Spectacular Foliage: Visit Bright or the Macedon Ranges for breathtaking autumn colors.
- Harvest Season: The Melbourne Food & Wine Festival takes center stage, celebrating local produce and culinary innovation.
- Hiking: Cooler weather makes it the perfect time to explore Grampians National Park and Wilson's Promontory.

Weather: Temperatures range from 10°C to 25°C (50°F to 77°F), offering mild and comfortable conditions.

Winter (June to August)
Best For: Snow adventures, cozy retreats, and cultural experiences
Winter transforms Victoria's alpine regions into snow-covered wonderlands, while the cities and countryside exude a cozy charm.
- Snow Sports: The Victorian High Country offers excellent skiing and snowboarding at resorts like Mount Buller and Falls Creek.
- City Escapes: Melbourne's Winter Night Markets and art exhibitions provide a warm cultural retreat.
- Indulgent Stays: Enjoy spa getaways in Daylesford, known for its mineral springs and luxurious accommodations.

Weather: Temperatures range from 5°C to 15°C (41°F to 59°F). Snowfall occurs in alpine areas, while the cities experience cold but manageable winters.

Spring (September to November)
Best For: Gardens, wildlife, and outdoor exploration
Spring breathes life into Victoria with blooming flowers, wildlife activity, and mild weather, making it a favorite for nature enthusiasts.

- Gardens in Bloom: Don't miss the Royal Botanic Gardens in Melbourne or the Tesselaar Tulip Festival.
- Wildlife Watching: Visit Phillip Island for the adorable penguin parade and Healesville Sanctuary for native wildlife encounters.
- Active Adventures: Ideal weather for cycling on the Murray to Mountains Rail Trail or kayaking on Lake Eildon.

Weather: Temperatures range from 15°C to 25°C (59°F to 77°F), with occasional spring showers.

Special Tips for 2025
- Avoid Peak Crowds: Summer and major event periods attract large crowds. Book accommodations early if traveling during these times.
- Flexible Travel: Victoria's weather can be unpredictable, especially in spring and autumn. Pack layers and rain gear to stay comfortable.
- Regional Events: Check for seasonal festivals in smaller towns, such as grape stomping in wine regions or food festivals in the countryside.

The Verdict
The best time to visit Victoria ultimately depends on your interests. For beach lovers and festival-goers, summer is perfect. If you're drawn to food, wine, and scenic beauty, consider autumn or spring.

Winter offers a cozy escape and snow adventures for those seeking a magical alpine experience. Whenever you decide to visit, Victoria's charm will ensure your trip is unforgettable.

Visa And Travel Requirements

Before embarking on your journey to Victoria, Australia, ensuring you meet the visa and travel requirements is a critical step in the planning process. Whether you're visiting for tourism, business, or a longer stay, understanding the formalities will help ensure a smooth and hassle-free experience.

Visa Requirements for International Travelers

Most travelers require a visa to enter Australia, including Victoria. The type of visa you need depends on the purpose and duration of your stay. Here's an overview of common visa options:

1. Visitor Visa (Subclass 600)
   - Designed for tourists and short-term visitors.
   - Valid for stays of up to 3, 6, or 12 months.
   - Can be applied for online.

2. Electronic Travel Authority (ETA) (Subclass 601)

- For passport holders from eligible countries, including the U.S., Canada, and several European nations.
- Allows stays of up to 3 months.
- Application is straightforward and done online or via the Australian ETA app.

3. eVisitor Visa (Subclass 651)
- Specifically for citizens of European Union member countries and some additional European nations.
- Free of charge and valid for up to 3 months per visit.

4. Working Holiday Visa (Subclass 417 or 462)
- For young travelers (aged 18–30 or 35 for some countries) wishing to travel and work temporarily in Australia.
- Allows stays of up to 12 months with work and travel flexibility.

Note: Always check the latest visa requirements and eligibility criteria on the [Australian Government Department of Home Affairs website](https://immi.homeaffairs.gov.au), as policies may change.

Documents Required for Visa Application

Prepare the following documents when applying for a visa:
- A valid passport with at least six months of validity from your intended travel date.
- Completed visa application form.
- Proof of funds to cover your stay, such as bank statements.
- Travel itinerary, including flight bookings and accommodation details.
- Health insurance (mandatory for some visa types).
- Letter of invitation (if applicable).

Travel Requirements: COVID-19 and Beyond
Australia has lifted most pandemic-related travel restrictions, but travelers should remain informed about current health and safety requirements.

1. Vaccination Requirements
- Travelers no longer need to show proof of COVID-19 vaccination unless otherwise stated.
- Ensure routine vaccinations, such as measles, mumps, and rubella (MMR), are up-to-date.

2. Health Insurance
- International visitors are encouraged to obtain comprehensive travel insurance covering medical emergencies, as healthcare costs in Australia can be high.

3. Quarantine Rules
   - Check for any quarantine or testing requirements closer to your travel date, as these may change with new health developments.

Customs and Biosecurity Regulations
Australia has strict biosecurity laws to protect its unique environment. Familiarize yourself with what you can and cannot bring into the country.
- Prohibited Items: Fresh food, plants, seeds, and animal products are restricted. Declare any of these items on your incoming passenger card.
- Duty-Free Limits: Visitors may bring a limited quantity of alcohol, tobacco, and goods duty-free.
- Medication: Carry prescription medications in their original packaging, along with a copy of the prescription.

Arrival Process at Victorian Airports
1. Immigration Clearance
   - Present your passport, visa, and completed Incoming Passenger Card.
   - Electronic passport gates (SmartGates) are available for eligible travelers for faster processing.

2. Customs and Biosecurity
   - Declare all goods as required; penalties apply for non-declaration of prohibited items.

3. Transport to Your Destination
   - Melbourne Airport (Tullamarine) is the main international gateway to Victoria.
   - Options for getting to the city include taxis, rideshares, shuttle buses, and the SkyBus, which offers frequent service to central Melbourne.

Tips for Hassle-Free Travel
- Apply Early: Visa processing times vary. Apply at least 4–6 weeks before your intended travel date.
- Keep Digital Copies: Have digital backups of important documents like your passport, visa, and insurance policy.
- Stay Updated: Regularly check government websites for updates on visa policies or health advisories.

By ensuring all your visa and travel requirements are in order, you'll be ready to explore the wonders of Victoria without interruptions. With a little preparation, your trip can be seamless and unforgettable.

Packing Tips

Packing smartly for Victoria ensures you're prepared to enjoy everything the state has to offer, from its bustling cities to its diverse landscapes. With varying climates and activities, it's essential to include a mix of essentials tailored to the time of year and your itinerary. Here's your comprehensive guide to packing for Victoria.

1. Clothing Essentials
Victoria's weather can be unpredictable, with all four seasons sometimes experienced in a single day. Layering is key to staying comfortable.

For Summer (December–February):
- Lightweight, breathable fabrics like cotton or linen.
- T-shirts, shorts, and summer dresses for warm days.
- A wide-brimmed hat, sunglasses, and sunscreen for sun protection.
- A light jacket or cardigan for cooler evenings.

For Autumn (March–May):
- Long-sleeved shirts and pants for mild days.
- A medium-weight jacket for crisp mornings and evenings.
- Comfortable walking shoes for exploring cities or hiking trails.

For Winter (June–August):
- Warm clothing, including thermal layers, sweaters, and a heavy coat.

- Gloves, a scarf, and a beanie for chilly outdoor excursions.
- Waterproof boots or sturdy shoes for rain-prone days.

<u>For Spring (September–November):</u>
- Similar to autumn, pack layers to adapt to fluctuating temperatures.
- A lightweight rain jacket or umbrella for occasional spring showers.

2. Outdoor and Activity-Specific Gear

Victoria offers a mix of outdoor adventures, from hiking in national parks to relaxing on beaches. Pack accordingly:

- Hiking and Nature:
    - Comfortable, sturdy hiking shoes or boots.
    - Quick-dry clothing and moisture-wicking socks.
    - A daypack, reusable water bottle, and snacks.
    - Sunscreen and insect repellent.

- Beach Trips:
    - Swimwear, a beach towel, and flip-flops.
    - A rash guard for sun protection during water activities.
    - Snorkeling gear (optional) if visiting spots like Portsea or Wilsons Promontory.

- Alpine Adventures:
  - For trips to snowfields like Mount Buller or Falls Creek, bring snow gear, including waterproof pants and jackets, insulated gloves, and thermal socks.
  - Sunglasses or goggles to protect against glare.

3. Travel Essentials

Victoria's mix of urban and rural areas means you'll need some versatile travel items.
- A universal power adapter for Australian sockets (Type I).
- A portable phone charger and camera for capturing memories.
- A compact umbrella or foldable rain jacket.
- A reusable shopping bag for eco-friendly shopping.
- A secure crossbody bag or backpack for city exploring.

4. Seasonal Must-Haves

Victoria's seasons require some additional considerations:
- Summer: Reef-safe sunscreen, insect repellent, and a reusable water bottle to stay hydrated.
- Winter: Lip balm and moisturizer to combat dry skin caused by cold air.
- Spring and Autumn: Allergy medications if you're sensitive to pollen during spring blooms or autumn foliage.

5. Health and Safety Items
- A basic first-aid kit with band-aids, antiseptic wipes, and pain relievers.
- Prescription medications in original packaging, along with a copy of your prescription.
- Travel insurance details for emergencies.
- A face mask and hand sanitizer for hygiene.

6. Documents and Money
Keep these essentials organized and secure:
- Passport, visa, and printed copies of your itinerary.
- Driver's license or international driving permit if you plan to rent a car.
- Credit/debit cards and a small amount of Australian dollars for cash-only purchases.

7. Eco-Friendly Tips
Victoria is committed to sustainable tourism, so consider packing:
- A reusable coffee cup for takeaway drinks.
- Eco-friendly toiletries to reduce plastic waste.
- A refillable water bottle, as tap water is safe to drink in Victoria.

8. Optional Items for Comfort
- Noise-canceling headphones or earplugs for flights or train journeys.

- A travel pillow and lightweight blanket for long commutes.
- A guidebook or pre-downloaded maps and apps for navigating remote areas.

<u>Final Checklist</u>
1. Check the weather forecast for your travel dates to fine-tune your packing list.
2. Leave extra space in your suitcase for souvenirs like local wine, artwork, or hand-crafted items.
3. Remember luggage weight limits if flying domestically within Australia.

By packing thoughtfully, you'll be ready to fully embrace Victoria's dynamic landscapes, cultural vibrancy, and outdoor adventures. Whether you're hiking rugged trails, strolling Melbourne's laneways, or lounging on pristine beaches, you'll have everything you need for a memorable journey.

Chapter 3

SPENDING WISELY

Budgeting Your Trip

Victoria, Australia, offers a wide range of experiences for travelers with varying budgets. Whether you're looking for luxury indulgence or a cost-effective adventure, careful planning and budgeting will ensure your trip is both enjoyable and financially manageable. Here's how to make the most of your money while exploring the diverse landscapes, attractions, and cultures of Victoria.

1. Determine Your Travel Priorities
Start by identifying the experiences that matter most to you. Are you keen on visiting iconic landmarks like the Twelve Apostles or attending cultural

events in Melbourne? Understanding your priorities will help allocate your budget effectively.

- City vs. Countryside: Staying in Melbourne might require a higher accommodation and food budget, while rural areas may offer more affordable options.
- Activities: Some activities, like hiking in national parks, are free, while others, such as winery tours or ski trips, come with costs.

2. Budget for Major Expenses

Accommodation:

Victoria offers a variety of accommodation options to suit all budgets:
- Luxury: High-end hotels, boutique stays, and private villas in Melbourne or the Mornington Peninsula. Prices can range from AUD 300–800 per night.
- Mid-Range: Chain hotels, serviced apartments, and charming bed-and-breakfasts typically cost AUD 150–300 per night.
- Budget: Hostels, motels, or campgrounds are ideal for cost-conscious travelers, with prices starting at AUD 25–100 per night.

Transportation:

Getting around Victoria can be tailored to your budget:

- Car Rentals: A great option for exploring beyond Melbourne. Costs range from AUD 50–100 per day, excluding fuel and tolls.
- Public Transport: Melbourne's trains, trams, and buses are affordable, with daily passes (Myki card) costing around AUD 10. Regional trains to destinations like Ballarat or Geelong start at AUD 20 one-way.
- Tours: Guided day tours to attractions like the Great Ocean Road or Yarra Valley can cost AUD 100–200 per person.

Food and Dining:
Victoria's culinary scene caters to all budgets:
- Luxury Dining: High-end restaurants in Melbourne, such as fine-dining spots or degustation menus, can cost AUD 100–300 per meal.
- Mid-Range Dining: Pubs, cafes, and casual eateries offer meals for AUD 20–40.
- Budget Options: Food trucks, markets, or fast-food outlets provide meals for AUD 10–20.

Activities and Attractions:
Some activities in Victoria are free or low-cost, while others require budgeting:
- Free options: Exploring Melbourne's laneways, public gardens, and museums with free entry.

- Paid options: Entry fees for attractions like the Melbourne Zoo (AUD 42) or Sovereign Hill (AUD 45).

3. Tips for Saving Money
- Travel in the Shoulder Season: Visiting during autumn (March–May) or spring (September–November) avoids peak-season rates while enjoying pleasant weather.
- Use Public Transport in Melbourne: The city's extensive tram network is free in the central business district (CBD).
- Pack Your Own Food: For day trips or hikes, bringing snacks or a picnic can save money on dining out.
- Look for Deals and Discounts: Check local tourism websites or apps for discounts on tours, attractions, and dining. Groupon and similar platforms often have deals for Victoria-based experiences.

4. Consider Hidden Costs
Be prepared for expenses that might not immediately come to mind:
- Tolls: Many highways around Melbourne are tolled. Budget around AUD 15–20 for a day of driving.
- Parking Fees: Especially in Melbourne, parking can cost AUD 20–50 per day in the CBD.

- National Park Entry: Some parks, like Wilsons Promontory, have parking fees ranging from AUD 10–20.
- Travel Insurance: Essential for peace of mind, with costs typically around AUD 50–100 per trip.

5. Daily Budget Estimate
- Shoestring Budget: AUD 50–100 per day, relying on hostels, public transport, and self-catering.
- Mid-Range Budget: AUD 150–300 per day, staying in mid-tier accommodations and dining at cafes or pubs.
- Luxury Budget: AUD 500+ per day, enjoying premium stays, fine dining, and exclusive tours.

By planning your trip budget carefully, you can tailor your Victoria adventure to your financial comfort level. Whether you're splurging on luxury or finding creative ways to save, the state's diverse offerings ensure a fulfilling experience for every traveler.

Cost-Saving Tips

Exploring Victoria, Australia, doesn't have to break the bank. With thoughtful planning and strategic choices, you can experience the state's vibrant cities, stunning landscapes, and rich culture without overspending. Here are some practical cost-saving tips to help you maximize your trip while staying within budget.

1. Plan Your Trip in the Off-Season
- Travel During Shoulder Seasons: Visit in autumn (March–May) or spring (September–November) to avoid peak-season prices. Accommodation and activities are often more affordable, and the weather is still pleasant.
- Avoid Major Events: Events like the Australian Open or Melbourne Cup can drive up prices for hotels and transportation. Plan your trip around these dates to save.

2. Choose Budget-Friendly Accommodation
- Hostels and Budget Hotels: Hostels, motels, and budget hotels are widely available in Melbourne and regional towns, offering comfortable stays at reasonable prices.
- Campgrounds: If you're exploring areas like the Great Ocean Road or national parks, camping is an economical and scenic option.
- Stay Outside the CBD: Accommodations in Melbourne's suburbs are often cheaper than those in the central business district, with good public transport connections.

3. Use Public Transport

- Melbourne's Free Tram Zone: Take advantage of the free tram network within Melbourne's CBD to save on transportation costs.
- Myki Card: Use a Myki card for affordable access to Melbourne's trains, trams, and buses, with daily caps to limit expenses.
- Regional Transport: For trips outside Melbourne, regional buses and trains are often cheaper than renting a car. Book in advance for discounts.

4. Save on Food and Drinks
- Explore Food Markets: Visit places like the Queen Victoria Market for fresh, affordable produce and ready-to-eat meals.
- Dine at Pubs and Cafes: Many pubs offer meal deals, such as "parma and a pot" nights, where you get a hearty meal with a drink for a fixed price.
- Self-Cater: If you're staying in accommodation with kitchen facilities, prepare some meals yourself to cut dining expenses.
- Bring a Reusable Water Bottle: Tap water is safe to drink in Victoria, so refill your bottle instead of buying bottled water.

5. Look for Free and Low-Cost Activities
- Explore Free Attractions: Enjoy Melbourne's public gardens, street art laneways, and free-entry museums like the NGV Australia and ACMI.

- National Parks: Many parks, including the Dandenong Ranges and Grampians, have free entry, though some charge a small parking fee.
- Beach Days: Victoria's beaches, from St Kilda to Torquay, are free to visit and perfect for relaxing without spending a dime.

6. Find Discounts and Deals
- Tourism Passes: Look for multi-attraction passes that bundle entry fees at discounted rates, such as the Melbourne Attractions Pass.
- Book Ahead: Many attractions and tours offer early-bird discounts when booked online in advance.
- Coupons and Apps: Use platforms like Groupon or local tourism apps for deals on dining, activities, and accommodations.

7. Manage Transportation Costs
- Car Rentals: If you need a car for road trips, compare rental companies for the best rates and book early to secure discounts.
- Share Costs: Split car rental and fuel costs with travel companions if you're in a group.
- Avoid Tolls: Plan your routes to bypass toll roads, as fees can add up quickly.

8. Pack Smartly

- Avoid Buying Extras: Bring essentials like sunscreen, reusable shopping bags, and beach gear from home to avoid spending on overpriced tourist items.
- Weather-Appropriate Clothing: Victoria's weather can change quickly, so packing layers will save you from needing to purchase extra clothing.

9. Opt for Free Wi-Fi
- Use Free Hotspots: Many cafes, libraries, and public spaces in Melbourne offer free Wi-Fi, helping you save on mobile data costs.

10. Be Mindful of Hidden Costs
- Budget for Parking Fees: If driving, research parking options in advance to avoid high fees, especially in Melbourne.
- Bring Snacks: Carry your own snacks for day trips to avoid overpriced convenience store items.

By incorporating these cost-saving tips into your travel plans, you can enjoy the best of Victoria while keeping your expenses in check. Whether you're exploring urban Melbourne or adventuring through the state's natural wonders, you'll find countless ways to create unforgettable memories without overspending.

Best Value For Money Experiences

Victoria, Australia, is brimming with experiences that offer exceptional value for travelers seeking unforgettable moments without overspending. From free natural attractions to budget-friendly cultural experiences, here are some of the best value-for-money activities and destinations to explore in Victoria.

1. Explore Melbourne's Free Attractions
- Street Art in Melbourne's Laneways: Discover vibrant murals and graffiti art in iconic laneways like Hosier Lane and AC/DC Lane, all at no cost.
- Royal Botanic Gardens: Spend a tranquil day strolling through this expansive garden featuring native and exotic plant species, with free entry.
- NGV Australia: Enjoy free exhibitions showcasing Australian art at the National Gallery of Victoria's Federation Square location.

2. Take a Scenic Drive Along the Great Ocean Road
One of the world's most famous coastal drives, the Great Ocean Road offers jaw-dropping views, charming seaside towns, and natural wonders.
- Must-See Stops: The Twelve Apostles, Loch Ard Gorge, and London Arch are all free to visit.
- Pack a Picnic: Save on dining costs by enjoying a packed lunch at a scenic lookout.

3. Visit Victoria's National Parks

Victoria's national parks offer incredible opportunities for hiking, wildlife spotting, and photography, many with free or minimal entry fees.

- Wilsons Promontory: Known for its stunning beaches, granite peaks, and wildlife, this park has no entry fee.
- Grampians National Park: Explore dramatic rock formations, waterfalls, and Aboriginal rock art sites.
-Dandenong Ranges: Enjoy a peaceful escape close to Melbourne, with walking trails and scenic lookouts.

4. Immerse Yourself in Local Markets

Victoria's markets are perfect for soaking in the local culture while enjoying affordable food and unique finds.

- Queen Victoria Market (Melbourne): Sample international cuisines and shop for souvenirs.
- St Andrews Market: A community market near the Yarra Valley offering handmade crafts, fresh produce, and live music.
- Geelong's Waterfront Market: Combine market shopping with a day by the bay.

5. Indulge in Affordable Culinary Delights

Victoria's diverse food scene caters to all budgets, offering incredible value for foodies.

- Cheap Eats in Melbourne: Visit Chinatown for dumplings or grab a famous banh mi in Footscray.
- Regional Wineries: Many wineries in the Yarra Valley or Mornington Peninsula offer free or low-cost tastings with the purchase of a bottle.
- Food Festivals: Attend food and wine festivals where entry fees are minimal, and you can sample a variety of dishes at affordable prices.

6. Discover Historic Towns

Victoria's gold rush history is preserved in charming regional towns offering enriching experiences at reasonable costs.
- Ballarat: Visit Sovereign Hill, where you can pan for gold and explore a recreated 1850s town.
- Bendigo: Take a guided tour of the Central Deborah Gold Mine.
- Castlemaine: Wander through galleries, antique shops, and historical buildings for free or a small donation.

7. Enjoy Free or Low-Cost Beaches

Victoria's coastline is dotted with pristine beaches that are perfect for relaxation and adventure.
- St Kilda Beach: Enjoy a day by the water and watch the famous penguin parade at dusk for free.
- Bells Beach: Famous for its surf scene, it's an excellent spot to watch surfers or enjoy the rugged coastline.

- Brighton Beach: Take photos of the colorful bathing boxes or enjoy a leisurely swim.

8. Attend Festivals and Events
Victoria hosts numerous festivals throughout the year, many of which are free or inexpensive to attend.
- White Night Melbourne: Experience the city transformed with light projections, art installations, and performances.
- Moomba Festival: A free family-friendly festival with a carnival atmosphere along the Yarra River.
- Regional Events: Look for local fairs and markets in smaller towns for unique and affordable experiences.

9. Hop on a Free Tour or Experience
- Melbourne Free Walking Tours: Learn about the city's history, architecture, and culture on a pay-what-you-want walking tour.
- Australian Open Live Sites: During the tennis tournament, enjoy free entertainment and large-screen match viewings in public areas.
- Federation Square Events: Check the calendar for free exhibitions, film screenings, and live performances.

10. Take Advantage of Public Transport Deals

- Free Tram Zone: Use Melbourne's free tram network to explore the CBD and Docklands without spending a cent.
- Regional Train Journeys: Scenic train rides to destinations like Geelong or Ballarat are affordable and picturesque.

11. DIY Adventure Activities
- Hiking Trails: Explore scenic trails like the Great Ocean Walk or trails in the You Yangs for free.
- Cycling: Rent a bike or use Melbourne's bike-sharing services to tour the city on a budget.
- Wildlife Watching: Visit spots like Tower Hill Reserve or Phillip Island for encounters with native animals.

With these value-for-money experiences, you can uncover the best of Victoria without overspending. From free activities to budget-friendly attractions, the state offers a wealth of options for an unforgettable yet economical journey.

Chapter 4

GETTING AROUND

Transportation Options

Victoria, Australia, boasts a well-connected transportation network that makes exploring the state both convenient and enjoyable. Whether you're navigating the bustling streets of Melbourne or venturing into the countryside, there are a variety of options to suit different travel styles and budgets. Here's a comprehensive guide to getting around in Victoria.

1. Public Transport in Melbourne
Melbourne's public transport system is extensive, reliable, and affordable, providing easy access to the city and surrounding suburbs.

- Trains: Melbourne's train network connects the central business district (CBD) to outlying suburbs. Trains operate frequently, with services extending late into the night on weekends.
- Trams: Known for its iconic trams, Melbourne offers a Free Tram Zone in the CBD, allowing passengers to travel for free in the city center. Outside this zone, fares are affordable and charged via the Myki card system.
- Buses: Melbourne's buses complement the train and tram network, serving areas not covered by other modes of public transport.

How to Use Public Transport:
- Purchase a Myki card, a reusable travel card, to access trains, trams, and buses.
- Daily fare caps ensure you won't spend more than AUD 10.60 (or less for concession holders) on public transport in Melbourne.

2. Regional Public Transport
For destinations outside Melbourne, Victoria's regional transport options are efficient and budget-friendly.

- V/Line Trains and Buses: These services connect Melbourne to regional cities like Ballarat, Bendigo, Geelong, and beyond. V/Line buses extend the network to smaller towns and rural areas.

- Fares: Regional train fares are reasonable, with discounts for off-peak travel. Advance bookings are recommended during busy periods.

3. Driving and Car Rentals

Driving is one of the best ways to explore Victoria's diverse landscapes, particularly for attractions outside urban areas.

- Car Rentals: Rental cars are widely available in Melbourne and major regional cities. Prices start at approximately AUD 50–100 per day, with options ranging from economy cars to SUVs.
- Road Conditions: Victoria has well-maintained roads, and driving is on the left side. The state also has several toll roads in Melbourne, so consider adding a toll pass to your rental.
- Key Road Trips:
  - The Great Ocean Road: A scenic coastal drive featuring landmarks like the Twelve Apostles.
  - The Yarra Valley: A short drive from Melbourne, ideal for wine tours and hot air ballooning.
  - Grampians National Park: Perfect for nature lovers and hikers.

4. Cycling

Cycling is a popular and eco-friendly way to explore both urban and rural Victoria.

- Bike Paths in Melbourne: The city is bicycle-friendly, with dedicated bike lanes and paths like the Capital City Trail and the Yarra Trail.
- Bike Rentals: Bike-sharing services such as Lime or Bluebikes are widely available in Melbourne. Rates typically start from AUD 5 per hour.
- Regional Cycling: Rail trails, like the Great Victorian Rail Trail, offer scenic routes through vineyards, forests, and historic towns.

5. Guided Tours and Day Trips

For hassle-free exploration, consider guided tours or day trips to Victoria's top attractions.

- Bus Tours: Many operators offer day trips to popular destinations such as the Great Ocean Road, Yarra Valley, or Phillip Island. Prices range from AUD 100–200 per person, often including transportation, entry fees, and meals.
- Custom Tours: Private tours can be tailored to your interests, though they are typically more expensive.

6. Ridesharing and Taxis

For short trips or late-night travel, ridesharing and taxis are convenient options.

- Ridesharing: Services like Uber, Didi, and Ola operate in Melbourne and many regional areas. Fares are typically cheaper than traditional taxis.
- Taxis: Available throughout Victoria, but fares are higher compared to ridesharing. Look for marked taxi ranks in busy areas.

7. Ferries and Water Transport
Victoria's waterways offer unique transport options for certain destinations.

- Port Phillip Ferries: Travel between Docklands (Melbourne) and regional areas like Geelong or the Bellarine Peninsula by ferry.
- Sorrento to Queenscliff Ferry: A scenic and efficient way to cross Port Phillip Bay, ideal for travelers exploring both the Mornington Peninsula and Bellarine Peninsula.

8. Walking
Walking is an excellent way to explore Victoria's cities and natural attractions.
- Urban Walking: Melbourne's CBD is compact and easily walkable, with landmarks, laneways, and parks within close proximity.
- Hiking Trails: For nature enthusiasts, Victoria offers countless hiking opportunities, from Wilsons Promontory to the Grampians.

9. Tips for Getting Around in Victoria
- Plan Ahead: Check schedules and fares for public transport and regional services in advance.
- Travel Off-Peak: Avoid peak-hour travel to save on fares and enjoy a more relaxed journey.
- Pack for Comfort: Whether you're hiking, cycling, or walking, wear comfortable shoes and bring essentials like water and sunscreen.

By taking advantage of Victoria's diverse transportation options, you can explore every corner of this vibrant state with ease. From the convenience of public transport in Melbourne to the freedom of a road trip, there's a mode of travel to suit every itinerary and budget.

Driving In Victoria

Driving in Victoria offers unparalleled freedom to explore the state's diverse landscapes, from bustling cities to serene countryside and dramatic coastlines. Whether you're cruising along the iconic Great Ocean Road or venturing into wine regions and national parks, having a car unlocks access to many of Victoria's hidden gems. Here's everything you need to know about driving in Victoria.

1. Why Drive in Victoria?

- Flexibility and Freedom: Create your own itinerary and explore at your own pace.
- Scenic Routes: Victoria boasts some of Australia's most beautiful drives, including the Great Ocean Road, the Yarra Valley, and the Grampians.
- Access to Remote Areas: Public transport doesn't reach every corner of the state, making driving the best way to access remote attractions.

2. Driving Rules and Regulations
- Drive on the Left: In Victoria, and throughout Australia, driving is on the left side of the road.
- Speed Limits:
    - Urban areas: 50 km/h unless otherwise posted.
    - Highways: Typically 100–110 km/h.
- Seat Belts: Mandatory for all passengers.
- Mobile Phones: It is illegal to use a handheld mobile phone while driving. Use hands-free options if necessary.
- Drink Driving: The legal blood alcohol limit is 0.05%. Strict penalties apply for exceeding this limit.

3. Car Rentals in Victoria
- Rental Locations: Major car rental companies, such as Hertz, Avis, and Budget, operate in Melbourne and larger regional towns.
- Requirements:

- A valid driver's license, either in English or accompanied by an International Driving Permit.
- Drivers must typically be 21 or older, with a surcharge for drivers under 25.
- Cost:
  - Economy cars start at AUD 50–100 per day, with discounts for longer rentals.
  - Additional costs include insurance, tolls, and fuel.

4. Toll Roads
Victoria has several toll roads, mainly in Melbourne.
- How to Pay: Most toll roads operate electronically. Use a rental car's toll pass or pre-purchase a visitor's e-tag online.
- Avoiding Tolls: Plan routes to bypass toll roads if you want to save money, although this may add travel time.

5. Parking in Victoria
- Melbourne CBD: Parking in central Melbourne is limited and often expensive. Use parking apps like PayStay to find and pay for parking.
- Suburban and Regional Areas: Parking is more readily available and often free, though some attractions charge a small fee.

- National Parks: Car parks at major parks and attractions can fill quickly during peak seasons. Arrive early to secure a spot.

6. Road Conditions and Safety
- Urban Roads: Well-maintained, with clear signage. Be mindful of tram lanes and pedestrian crossings in Melbourne.
- Highways: High-quality roads connect major cities and towns. Watch for wildlife, especially at dawn and dusk.
- Rural Roads: Can be narrow and winding. Gravel or unsealed roads may require extra caution.

7. Scenic Drives to Explore
Victoria offers many iconic road trips and scenic routes:
- Great Ocean Road: A stunning coastal route with landmarks like the Twelve Apostles and Loch Ard Gorge.
- Yarra Valley: Rolling vineyards and charming villages, perfect for a day trip.
- Grampians National Park: Rugged mountain landscapes and Aboriginal rock art.
- Mornington Peninsula: Coastal scenery, wineries, and hot springs.
- High Country: Alpine roads leading to ski resorts in winter and hiking trails in summer.

8. Fuel and Gas Stations
- Fuel Types: Petrol (unleaded), diesel, and LPG are widely available. Check your rental car's fuel type before refueling.
- Cost: Petrol prices fluctuate, averaging around AUD 1.80–2.10 per liter. Use fuel apps like Petrol Spy to find the cheapest fuel nearby.
- Availability: Gas stations are plentiful in urban and suburban areas but can be sparse in remote regions. Plan refueling stops accordingly.

9. Preparing for Long Drives
- Navigation: Use GPS or apps like Google Maps or Waze. Download offline maps for areas with limited signal.
- Rest Stops: Take breaks every two hours during long drives. Victoria's highways have rest areas with toilets and picnic facilities.
- Emergency Kit: Pack essentials like water, snacks, a first aid kit, and a phone charger.

10. Wildlife and Road Hazards
- Kangaroos and Other Wildlife: Wildlife is more active at dawn, dusk, and night. Drive cautiously in rural areas to avoid collisions.
- Weather Conditions:
  - In winter, roads in alpine regions may be icy or require snow chains.

- Check weather forecasts for updates on conditions.

11. Insurance and Roadside Assistance
- Rental Insurance: Most car rentals include basic insurance, but consider purchasing additional coverage for peace of mind.
- Roadside Assistance: Many rental companies offer roadside assistance. Ensure you have the emergency contact details before heading out.

12. Eco-Friendly Driving Tips
- Carpooling: Share rides with friends or other travelers to reduce fuel consumption.
- Plan Efficient Routes: Minimize unnecessary driving to save fuel and lower emissions.
- Respect Nature: Stay on designated roads and parking areas to protect the environment.

Driving in Victoria is an adventure in itself, providing the freedom to explore iconic attractions and discover off-the-beaten-path treasures. With the right preparation and awareness of road rules, you'll enjoy a safe and memorable journey through this remarkable state.

Navigating Public Transit

Public transit in Victoria is an efficient and budget-friendly way to explore the region, particularly in Melbourne and its surrounding suburbs. The network consists of trains, trams, and buses, making it possible to travel with ease whether you're commuting within the city or heading to nearby attractions.

Melbourne's trams are iconic and form the backbone of the city's public transport system. The Free Tram Zone in the central business district (CBD) allows passengers to hop on and off without paying, making it ideal for tourists exploring key landmarks such as Federation Square, the Melbourne Museum, and the Queen Victoria Market. Trams outside the Free Tram Zone require a Myki card, the ticketing system for all public transport in Victoria.

The train network in Melbourne extends from the CBD to suburban areas, with multiple lines departing from major hubs like Flinders Street Station and Southern Cross Station. Trains run frequently during the day and provide late-night services on weekends. For regional travel, V/Line trains connect Melbourne with cities like Ballarat, Bendigo, Geelong, and beyond, offering a comfortable and scenic journey.

Buses in Victoria complement the train and tram network by servicing areas that other modes do not cover. They are particularly useful for reaching destinations in outer suburbs or for early morning and late-night travel. The bus routes also connect to major train stations, ensuring smooth transitions between different modes of transport.

Using public transit requires a Myki card, which can be purchased and topped up at train stations, convenience stores, and online. The card allows seamless travel across trams, trains, and buses, with fare caps ensuring a maximum daily expenditure. Children, seniors, and concession cardholders receive discounted fares.

Public transport operates on a reliable schedule, but planning is essential for smooth travel. Apps like PTV (Public Transport Victoria) provide real-time updates, route planning, and timetable information. These tools are invaluable for navigating unfamiliar routes and ensuring timely connections.

In regional areas, the public transport system is less extensive but still efficient for key routes. V/Line buses and trains are the primary modes of transit, connecting smaller towns and regional centers. These services require advance booking during peak times to secure a seat, particularly for popular tourist destinations.

Accessibility features are incorporated across the network, including low-floor trams, wheelchair-accessible buses, and elevators at train stations. This ensures inclusivity for travelers with mobility challenges.

Public transport in Victoria offers an affordable and convenient way to explore the state. Whether you're riding a tram in Melbourne or taking a scenic train journey to regional attractions, the system ensures a hassle-free experience for visitors and locals alike.

Chapter 5

WHERE TO STAY

Accommodation Types

Victoria offers a wide range of accommodation options to suit every type of traveler, budget, and itinerary. From luxury hotels to charming countryside retreats, there's something for everyone.

Hotels are a popular choice for travelers seeking comfort and convenience. Melbourne, as the state's capital, is home to an array of international hotel chains, boutique establishments, and mid-range options. Many hotels are located in the central business district (CBD), providing easy access to major attractions, dining, and shopping. Outside Melbourne, regional cities like Geelong, Ballarat, and Bendigo also feature excellent hotel options with a mix of modern amenities and historical charm.

Serviced apartments are ideal for families, groups, or travelers on extended stays. These accommodations provide the comforts of home, including kitchen facilities and laundry services, while offering the convenience of a hotel. They are commonly found in Melbourne and larger regional towns.

For those seeking unique and luxurious experiences, boutique accommodations and bed-and-breakfasts offer personalized service and a more intimate atmosphere. Many are located in scenic areas such as the Yarra Valley, Mornington Peninsula, and the Great Ocean Road, where guests can enjoy gourmet breakfasts, local wines, and stunning views.

Budget travelers will find plenty of affordable options, including hostels and motels. Hostels are perfect for backpackers and solo travelers, providing shared dormitory-style rooms, private rooms, and communal facilities. Motels, often situated along highways or in small towns, offer simple, cost-effective lodging for road trippers and those passing through.

Victoria's countryside and natural attractions are home to a variety of charming cottages, cabins, and farm stays. These accommodations allow visitors to immerse themselves in rural life, offering cozy lodgings surrounded by vineyards, rolling hills, or bushland. Some farm stays even include opportunities to interact with animals or learn about local agriculture.

For nature enthusiasts, campgrounds and caravan parks provide a great way to enjoy Victoria's outdoor beauty. Parks in areas such as the Grampians, Wilsons Promontory, and the Otways offer facilities for tents, campervans, and caravans. Many also feature cabins for those seeking a more comfortable outdoor experience.

Luxury resorts and spas cater to travelers looking for indulgence and relaxation. From the hot springs of the Mornington Peninsula to the high-end retreats of Daylesford and Hepburn Springs, these destinations offer world-class service, spa treatments, and breathtaking natural surroundings.

Vacation rentals, including holiday homes and apartments, are another excellent option for travelers seeking flexibility and privacy. Platforms like Airbnb and Stayz offer properties ranging from city apartments to beachside houses, accommodating small groups to large families.

No matter your budget or travel style, Victoria provides a diverse array of accommodations. From the vibrant streets of Melbourne to the tranquil countryside, every visitor can find the perfect place to rest and recharge while exploring this remarkable state.

Top Hotels And Hostels

Victoria boasts an impressive selection of accommodations, from opulent hotels to budget-friendly hostels. Here's a curated list of some of the best places to stay, catering to various tastes and budgets.

Hotels
1. The Langham, Melbourne
   - Location: Southbank, Melbourne
   - Highlights: Renowned for its luxurious rooms, riverfront location, and exceptional service, The Langham is perfect for travelers seeking elegance and comfort. Its proximity to Crown Casino and the National Gallery of Victoria makes it a prime choice for exploring Melbourne's attractions.

2. Park Hyatt Melbourne

- Location: East Melbourne
- Highlights: Nestled near Fitzroy Gardens, this five-star hotel offers sophisticated accommodations with a focus on wellness. Guests can enjoy spacious suites, an indoor pool, and a tranquil day spa.

3. Sofitel Melbourne on Collins
   - Location: Melbourne CBD
   - Highlights: This upscale hotel boasts breathtaking city views, modern décor, and exceptional dining at No35 restaurant. Its location on Collins Street is ideal for shopping and cultural experiences.

4. Lake House, Daylesford
   - Location: Daylesford
   - Highlights: A luxurious retreat in Victoria's spa country, the Lake House combines fine dining with boutique accommodations. It's an excellent choice for those seeking relaxation and a connection with nature.

5. Jackalope Hotel, Mornington Peninsula
   - Location: Merricks North
   - Highlights: This award-winning hotel merges striking modern design with vineyard views. Guests can enjoy wine tastings, gourmet dining, and an infinity pool overlooking the rolling hills.

6. Vue Grand, Queenscliff
 - Location: Queenscliff
 - Highlights: A historic hotel offering a blend of heritage charm and modern amenities. Its coastal location makes it a favorite for exploring the Bellarine Peninsula.

Hostels
1. Space Hotel
 - Location: Melbourne CBD
 - Highlights: A modern hostel that feels like a boutique hotel, Space Hotel features comfortable dorms and private rooms, a rooftop terrace with city views, and a cinema room. It's ideal for budget-conscious travelers who want style and convenience.

2. Base Backpackers St Kilda
 - Location: St Kilda, Melbourne
 - Highlights: Known for its vibrant atmosphere, Base Backpackers is close to the beach and St Kilda's nightlife. It's perfect for young travelers looking to socialize and enjoy Melbourne's seaside culture.

3. YHA Melbourne Central
 - Location: Melbourne CBD
 - Highlights: A centrally located hostel offering clean, affordable accommodations with a rooftop

terrace, communal kitchen, and regular social events. It's ideal for backpackers exploring Melbourne's urban delights.

4. Halls Gap YHA Eco-Hostel
   - Location: Halls Gap, Grampians National Park
   - Highlights: An eco-friendly hostel set in stunning natural surroundings. It's perfect for travelers seeking outdoor adventures like hiking, rock climbing, and wildlife spotting.

5. Apollo Bay Eco YHA
   - Location: Apollo Bay, Great Ocean Road
   - Highlights: Situated along the Great Ocean Road, this eco-hostel provides comfortable lodgings with sustainable features. It's a great base for exploring the Twelve Apostles and Otway Rainforest.

6. The Nunnery
   - Location: Fitzroy, Melbourne
   - Highlights: A unique hostel in a converted convent, The Nunnery offers charm, character, and a prime location near Melbourne's eclectic Fitzroy district.

Whether you're after luxury or affordability, Victoria's top hotels and hostels provide excellent bases for discovering the state's many wonders.

Choose according to your style, budget, and desired location to make your stay unforgettable.

Unique Stays

Victoria offers a variety of unique and unconventional accommodations for travelers seeking something a bit different. From staying in a vineyard cabin to glamping under the stars, these options allow you to immerse yourself in the state's natural beauty and distinct charm.

1. Treehouse Accommodation in the Otways
   - Location: Otway Ranges, Great Ocean Road
   - Highlights: Escape to the treetops with a stay in a secluded treehouse nestled in the lush forests of the Otways. These eco-friendly stays often feature panoramic views, cozy interiors, and the sounds of nature surrounding you. Perfect for couples or those seeking solitude in the heart of nature.

2. Glamping at Grampians Eco YHA
   - Location: Halls Gap, Grampians National Park
   - Highlights: For a luxurious camping experience, try glamping in the Grampians. This unique stay offers canvas tents with real beds, air conditioning, and en-suite bathrooms, blending the outdoors with comfort. With spectacular mountain views and

nearby hiking trails, it's a perfect choice for adventure lovers.

3. Historic Lighthouse Stays
   - Location: Various locations along the coast (e.g., Cape Otway Lighthouse, Point Lonsdale Lighthouse)
   - Highlights: Sleep in a historic lighthouse and enjoy stunning ocean views. Many lighthouses in Victoria offer accommodation within the lighthouse keeper's cottages, providing a fascinating glimpse into maritime history. Experience the rugged coastline at sunrise or sunset and feel like you're truly off the beaten path.

4. Luxury Wine Retreats in the Yarra Valley
   - Location: Yarra Valley
   - Highlights: Stay in a luxury retreat set within the rolling hills of one of Victoria's premier wine regions. Many vineyard properties offer boutique accommodations where you can enjoy wine tastings, gourmet dining, and relaxing spa treatments. With stunning views of the vineyards and valley, it's an ideal getaway for wine enthusiasts.

5. Underground Accommodation at Coober Pedy
   - Location: Coober Pedy (though technically in South Australia, it's close to the Victorian border)

- Highlights: If you're willing to venture just outside Victoria, Coober Pedy offers unique underground stays in dugout homes, originally designed to escape the extreme heat. Experience life below the earth's surface with comfortable, modern amenities while staying cool in the heat of the outback.

6. Floating Hotels on Lake Eildon
  - Location: Lake Eildon, near Mansfield
  - Highlights: Stay on the water in a floating houseboat, offering a peaceful and private experience on the scenic Lake Eildon. Houseboats come equipped with kitchens, bathrooms, and spacious decks for outdoor dining, providing a tranquil way to explore the lake and nearby national parks.

7. Former Jail Accommodation in Beechworth
  - Location: Beechworth
  - Highlights: For a truly memorable experience, stay in a converted prison at the Beechworth Historic Precinct. The former jail offers overnight stays in re-purposed cells, allowing visitors to step back in time while still enjoying modern amenities. The site also includes a museum, making it a fascinating choice for history buffs.

8. Coastal Cabins at Wilsons Promontory

- Location: Wilsons Promontory National Park
 - Highlights: Stay in eco-friendly cabins at the southernmost tip of mainland Australia, surrounded by pristine beaches and dense forests. These cabins provide a secluded retreat perfect for hiking, wildlife watching, and soaking in the unspoiled beauty of one of Victoria's most loved national parks.

9. Vintage Caravans by the Beach in Gippsland
 - Location: Gippsland, Lakes Entrance
 - Highlights: For something truly quirky, stay in a restored vintage caravan parked by the beach. These nostalgic stays combine comfort and charm, often featuring bright retro décor, small kitchens, and outdoor decks with views of the sea. It's a fun way to experience coastal Victoria with a sense of nostalgia and comfort.

10. Homesteads on the High Country
 - Location: Victoria's High Country (e.g., Bright, Mount Buller, Beechworth)
 - Highlights: Stay in a charming country homestead, offering a serene and luxurious escape amidst Victoria's alpine and rural landscapes. Many homesteads feature expansive grounds, outdoor fireplaces, and cozy interiors, perfect for a winter getaway or a peaceful retreat in the warmer months.

Whether you're looking for a peaceful retreat in nature, a historic experience, or a quirky adventure, Victoria's unique stays offer something for everyone. From luxury vineyards to old lighthouses and floating hotels, these accommodations provide memorable experiences that go beyond the ordinary hotel stay.

Chapter 6

FOOD AND DRINK

Victoria's Culinary Scene

Melbourne, often hailed as Australia's culinary capital, is home to a dizzying array of restaurants, cafes, and food markets. Its multicultural population is reflected in its cuisine, with neighborhoods specializing in specific international flavors. In Carlton, savor authentic Italian pasta and pizza; in Richmond, explore the vibrant Vietnamese food scene; and in Footscray, enjoy African-inspired dishes. Melbourne's iconic laneways are dotted with hidden eateries offering unique dining experiences, while high-end establishments like Attica and Vue de Monde redefine gourmet dining with innovative techniques and local ingredients.

Regional Flavors and Local Produce
Victoria's regions are rich in fresh produce, offering visitors the chance to indulge in farm-to-table cuisine. The Mornington Peninsula and the Yarra Valley are known for their orchards, vineyards, and artisan products like cheeses, olive oils, and chocolates. Many restaurants in these regions partner with local farms to create seasonal menus that celebrate Victoria's natural bounty.

The Great Ocean Road and Gippsland regions are renowned for their seafood, including fresh oysters, crayfish, and abalone. Coastal towns such as Apollo Bay and Lakes Entrance offer waterside dining where you can enjoy the catch of the day with stunning ocean views.

Wine and Craft Beverages
Victoria's wine regions are among the best in Australia. The Yarra Valley is famous for its cool-climate wines, especially Chardonnay and Pinot Noir. A visit to this region is not complete without a wine-tasting tour of its celebrated vineyards, such as Domaine Chandon or TarraWarra Estate.

The Mornington Peninsula and the Grampians are also prominent wine regions, producing exceptional Shiraz and sparkling wines. For those who prefer beer and cider, Victoria's craft breweries and cideries offer unique, locally brewed beverages. Regions like the High Country are well-known for their craft beer trails, where visitors can sample everything from hoppy IPAs to refreshing ciders made with local apples and pears.

Coffee Culture
Victoria is synonymous with excellent coffee, and Melbourne leads the way as one of the world's coffee capitals. The city's obsession with the perfect cup has given rise to countless specialty cafes and skilled baristas. Visitors can explore Melbourne's vibrant coffee culture through its laneway cafes, coffee roasteries, and espresso bars. Popular spots like Seven Seeds, St. Ali, and Market Lane Coffee are must-visits for coffee aficionados.

Food Markets and Festivals
Victoria's food markets are a celebration of local flavors and community spirit. The Queen Victoria Market in Melbourne is an iconic destination, offering everything from fresh produce and gourmet ingredients to international street food. Other markets, such as the South Melbourne Market and Prahran Market, are also worth exploring for their variety and vibrant atmosphere.

Victoria's calendar is packed with food and drink festivals that showcase the state's culinary excellence. The Melbourne Food and Wine Festival draws foodies from around the globe to experience masterclasses, tastings, and pop-up dining events. Regional festivals, such as the Grampians Grape Escape and the King Valley's La Dolce Vita, offer immersive experiences in Victoria's wine and produce regions.

Unique Culinary Experiences
For a truly unforgettable experience, try dining aboard the Colonial Tramcar Restaurant in Melbourne, where you can enjoy a gourmet meal while gliding through the city streets. Alternatively, indulge in a multi-course meal at one of Victoria's eco-lodges, where the menu is tailored to highlight the freshest local ingredients.

Victoria's culinary scene is more than just food and drink—it's a journey of flavors, traditions, and creativity. Whether you're exploring the laneways of Melbourne, dining by the ocean, or sipping wine in the countryside, Victoria offers a feast for the senses.

Must-try Local Dishes

Victoria's culinary landscape is as diverse as its scenery, offering a mix of traditional Australian flavors, multicultural influences, and regional specialties. Here's a guide to the must-try dishes that capture the essence of Victoria's food culture.

1. Meat Pie

A quintessential Australian snack, the meat pie is a must-try in Victoria. These flaky pastries, filled with minced meat, gravy, and seasonings, can be found at bakeries, cafes, and even high-end restaurants. Try one from Footscray's Pie Thief or a gourmet twist at Pure Pie in Melbourne.

2. Parma (Chicken Parmigiana)

A pub classic, the chicken parmigiana (fondly called "parma") is a breaded chicken schnitzel topped with tomato sauce, melted cheese, and often served with chips and salad. Many pubs in Melbourne and regional Victoria take pride in their versions, making it a staple for both locals and visitors.

3. Flat White

No visit to Victoria is complete without indulging in its famous coffee culture. The flat white—a perfectly balanced combination of espresso and velvety steamed milk—is a staple in cafes across the state. Enjoy a cup at Melbourne institutions like Market Lane Coffee or Seven Seeds.

4. Dim Sims

An Australian take on traditional dim sum, dim sims (or "dimmies") originated in Melbourne. These oversized dumplings, usually filled with pork and vegetables, are steamed or fried and served hot. Sample them at South Melbourne Market, where they've been a favorite for decades.

5. Barramundi

As one of Australia's most iconic fish, barramundi is a popular menu item in Victoria. Grilled, pan-fried, or baked, it's typically served with a side of seasonal vegetables or a refreshing salad. Many seaside restaurants along the Great Ocean Road serve fresh barramundi with stunning coastal views.

6. Victorian Lamb

Victoria is renowned for its high-quality lamb, and dishes featuring this tender, flavorful meat are a culinary highlight. Look for slow-cooked lamb shanks, roasted lamb with herbs, or lamb cutlets at fine dining restaurants like Cutler & Co. or country pubs in regional towns.

7. Vegemite on Toast

A cultural icon of Australia, Vegemite is a salty, umami-rich spread that might be an acquired taste but is worth trying. Many cafes offer it as part of a classic Australian breakfast, served on buttered toast. Pair it with a coffee for the ultimate Aussie morning experience.

8. Fresh Oysters and Crayfish
Victoria's coastal regions, particularly Gippsland and Lakes Entrance, are celebrated for their fresh seafood. Enjoy plump, briny oysters on the half shell or indulge in the sweet, succulent flavors of local crayfish, often grilled with garlic butter.

9. Pavlova
This iconic dessert, featuring a crisp meringue shell with a soft marshmallow-like center, is topped with whipped cream and fresh fruit like strawberries, kiwi, and passionfruit. While it's popular across Australia, many Victorian bakeries and restaurants offer standout versions of this sweet treat.

10. Artisanal Cheese and Charcuterie
Victoria's Yarra Valley and Mornington Peninsula are renowned for their cheesemakers and charcuterie artisans. Sample creamy brie, sharp cheddar, and goat cheese paired with locally made cured meats, fresh bread, and regional wines. Many

cellar doors and markets offer tastings and ready-to-eat platters.

11. Lamingtons
A beloved Australian dessert, lamingtons are sponge cakes coated in chocolate and rolled in shredded coconut. Some versions are filled with cream or jam for extra decadence. Grab one at a local bakery or a specialty cafe in Melbourne.

12. Kangaroo Fillet
For adventurous eaters, kangaroo meat is a lean, flavorful option that is often grilled or pan-seared and served with native herbs and vegetables. Many upscale restaurants in Victoria feature it on their menus as a uniquely Australian experience.

13. Tim Tams
While technically a snack rather than a dish, Tim Tams are an Australian obsession. These chocolate-covered biscuits are best enjoyed with a hot drink. Try a "Tim Tam Slam," where you sip your coffee or tea through the biscuit like a straw, for a fun and indulgent treat.

14. Scones with Jam and Cream
High tea is a delightful tradition in Victoria, and scones with jam and cream are the stars. Soft, fluffy scones are served with locally made berry jams and

fresh clotted cream, a must-try at tea rooms like The Windsor Hotel in Melbourne.

15. Chiko Roll
Inspired by Chinese spring rolls but uniquely Australian, the Chiko Roll is a deep-fried snack filled with beef, barley, carrots, and cabbage. It's a popular takeaway item that's perfect for a quick bite on the go.

Whether you're sampling seafood by the coast, indulging in Melbourne's café culture, or exploring regional delicacies, Victoria's must-try dishes promise a culinary journey that's as diverse and exciting as the state itself.

Wine And Coffee Culture

Victoria is a paradise for wine enthusiasts and coffee aficionados alike, offering some of the finest vineyards and coffee roasters in the world. Whether you're savoring a cool-climate Pinot Noir in the Yarra Valley or enjoying a perfectly brewed flat white in Melbourne, the state's deep appreciation for quality beverages makes it a destination to remember.

Victoria's Wine Culture
Victoria boasts over 800 wineries spread across its picturesque regions, each offering a unique expression of the state's diverse climates and terrains.

- Yarra Valley:

The Yarra Valley is Victoria's most famous wine region, known for its cool-climate wines, particularly Chardonnay and Pinot Noir. Visitors can enjoy cellar door tastings at celebrated wineries like Domaine Chandon, TarraWarra Estate, and De Bortoli Wines. Many wineries also feature farm-to-table restaurants, making it an ideal spot for food and wine pairings.

- Mornington Peninsula:

This region produces exceptional sparkling wines and Pinot Gris. Its proximity to the coast means you can pair your wine tasting with breathtaking ocean views. Many vineyards, such as Montalto and Red Hill Estate, offer al fresco dining in idyllic settings.

- Grampians:
Known for its robust Shiraz, the Grampians is one of Victoria's oldest wine regions. Visit Seppelt Wines or Best's Wines to explore historic vineyards and underground cellars.

- Rutherglen:
Rutherglen is famous for its fortified wines, particularly Muscat and Tokay. A visit here promises rich, sweet flavors and a chance to explore the rustic charm of small, family-owned wineries.

- King Valley:
Nicknamed "Little Italy," the King Valley specializes in Italian varietals like Prosecco, Sangiovese, and Nebbiolo. Enjoy a glass of sparkling Prosecco while soaking in the lush valley views.

Victoria's wine regions aren't just about the wine. They often include opportunities for scenic drives, hot air balloon rides, and vineyard tours, making them perfect for a full-day or weekend getaway.

Melbourne's Coffee Culture
Melbourne is globally renowned for its coffee culture, and for good reason. The city's love affair with coffee is deeply ingrained in its daily life, with

an emphasis on quality, craftsmanship, and community.

- Specialty Cafes:
Melbourne's laneways are dotted with specialty cafes, each striving to perfect the art of coffee. From rich espressos to smooth lattes, Melbourne's cafes are destinations in themselves. Iconic spots include Seven Seeds, Proud Mary, and Market Lane Coffee, where the focus is on ethically sourced beans and precision brewing.

- Flat White Excellence:
The flat white, a silky blend of espresso and microfoam milk, is Melbourne's signature coffee. Many locals claim Melbourne makes the best flat whites in the world, and no visit is complete without trying one.

- Barista Skills and Latte Art:
Melbourne's baristas are considered some of the most skilled globally, often turning your coffee into a canvas with intricate latte art. Their dedication to creating the perfect cup is evident in every sip.

- Coffee Roasteries:
Many cafes in Melbourne also roast their own beans, ensuring freshness and offering blends unique to each establishment. Roasteries like Axil

Coffee Roasters and Code Black Coffee offer tours and tastings for coffee enthusiasts eager to learn more.

The Perfect Pairing: Wine and Coffee Experiences
Victoria provides unique experiences where wine and coffee intersect. Many boutique wineries have embraced coffee culture, offering gourmet coffee alongside their wines. Similarly, urban establishments in Melbourne often pair coffee tastings with dessert wines or liqueurs for a memorable culinary treat.

Events and Tours
- Melbourne Coffee Week:
 Held annually, this festival celebrates everything coffee, with workshops, tastings, and opportunities to meet local roasters.

- Wine Festivals:
 Events like the Melbourne Food and Wine Festival and the Grampians Grape Escape celebrate Victoria's wine heritage, offering tastings, masterclasses, and food pairings.

Whether you're exploring the rolling vineyards of the Yarra Valley or savoring a cup of coffee in a bustling Melbourne laneway, Victoria's wine and coffee cultures offer unforgettable experiences that reflect the state's passion for quality and creativity.

Chapter 7

ADVENTURES AND ACTIVITIES

Outdoor Adventures

Victoria's diverse landscapes provide an unparalleled playground for outdoor enthusiasts, offering everything from rugged coastlines and lush forests to alpine regions and arid deserts. Whether you're seeking adrenaline-pumping thrills or peaceful communion with nature, Victoria has adventures to suit every traveler.

Explore the Great Ocean Road

One of Australia's most iconic road trips, the Great Ocean Road is a must-do for adventure seekers. Along its winding route, visitors can enjoy activities such as:

- Surfing: Head to Bells Beach, a world-famous surfing destination, to ride the waves or watch professionals in action.
- Hiking: The Great Ocean Walk offers breathtaking coastal views, with trails passing through rainforests, cliffs, and secluded beaches.
- Kayaking and Snorkeling: At Apollo Bay, explore marine life in crystal-clear waters or kayak around sheltered coves.

Grampians National Park
The Grampians are a haven for hiking, rock climbing, and wildlife spotting. Adventurous activities here include:
- Hiking Trails: Popular hikes like the Pinnacle Walk and Mackenzie Falls provide stunning views of rugged mountain landscapes.
- Rock Climbing: The park is renowned for its world-class climbing spots, with challenges for both beginners and experienced climbers.
- Aboriginal Culture: Join guided tours to learn about the rich Indigenous history and view ancient rock art sites.

Phillip Island Adventures
Phillip Island combines wildlife experiences with water-based adventures. Visitors can enjoy:
- Penguin Parade: Witness the magical sight of little penguins waddling ashore at sunset.

- Wildlife Encounters: Koalas, seals, and native birds can be spotted at the island's nature parks.
- Water Sports: Try paddleboarding, jet skiing, or kite surfing along the island's pristine beaches.

High Country Escapades
Victoria's alpine region is perfect for year-round outdoor activities:
- Skiing and Snowboarding: In winter, Mount Hotham and Falls Creek transform into snowy playgrounds.
- Mountain Biking: Summer offers thrilling bike trails, such as the Epic Trail at Mount Buller.
- Horseback Riding: Experience the beauty of the Victorian Alps on horseback, reminiscent of Australia's iconic mountain cattlemen.

Dandenong Ranges
For those seeking adventure close to Melbourne, the Dandenong Ranges offer:
- Hiking Trails: Explore trails like the 1000 Steps Kokoda Track Memorial Walk for a blend of fitness and history.
- Ziplining: Soar through the treetops on zipline adventures that provide unique perspectives of the lush rainforest.
- Puffing Billy Railway: While not extreme, this steam train ride through picturesque landscapes is a charming outdoor experience.

Wilson's Promontory National Park

"Wilsons Prom" is a natural wonderland at the southernmost tip of mainland Australia. Adventurous visitors can:
- Hike to Mount Oberon: A rewarding trek offering panoramic views of beaches and islands.
- Camping: Pitch a tent under the stars at one of the park's campgrounds.
- Water Adventures: Snorkeling and diving in the marine national park reveal colorful coral reefs and diverse marine life.

Murray River Adventures

The Murray River provides a mix of relaxation and active pursuits:
- Paddling: Kayak or canoe through tranquil waters surrounded by lush riverbanks.
- Houseboating: Rent a houseboat for a unique adventure combining travel and comfort.
- Fishing: The river is known for its abundant Murray cod, making it a favorite for anglers.

Adventure on the Water

Victoria's coastline and inland waterways offer countless water-based activities:
- Scuba Diving: Explore shipwrecks and marine parks, such as the Port Phillip Heads Marine National Park.

- Whale Watching: During migration seasons, spot humpback whales off the coast at Warrnambool or Portland.
- Stand-Up Paddleboarding: Calm bays like those at the Mornington Peninsula are perfect for paddleboarding.

The You Yangs and Brisbane Ranges
Located near Geelong, these regions are perfect for outdoor enthusiasts:
- Mountain Biking: The You Yangs offer well-maintained trails with varying difficulty levels.
- Wildlife Walks: Spot kangaroos, koalas, and other native animals in the Brisbane Ranges.

Hot Air Ballooning Over the Yarra Valley
For a serene yet exhilarating adventure, take a hot air balloon ride over the Yarra Valley. Drift over vineyards and rolling hills as the sun rises, creating unforgettable memories.

The Otways
The Great Otway National Park is a lush paradise for nature lovers:
- Tree Top Walks: The Otway Fly Treetop Walk provides a bird's-eye view of the rainforest canopy.
- Waterfalls: Visit Erskine Falls or Hopetoun Falls for a refreshing and scenic trek.

Victoria's rich diversity of landscapes ensures there's no shortage of outdoor adventures. Whether you prefer scaling mountains, exploring underwater worlds, or enjoying tranquil rivers, the state promises unforgettable experiences for every type of adventurer.

Art, Culture, And Festivals

Victoria is a cultural hub, renowned for its vibrant arts scene, rich history, and an array of festivals that celebrate everything from food and music to film and fashion. Visitors exploring the state will find that its cultural offerings are just as adventurous as its landscapes, providing immersive and unforgettable experiences.

Melbourne's Art Scene

Melbourne, Victoria's capital, is the heart of the state's artistic expression, offering a dynamic mix of contemporary and traditional art.
- Street Art: Melbourne's laneways, particularly Hosier Lane, are famous for their colorful, ever-changing street art. Stroll through these alleyways to discover large-scale murals, intricate graffiti, and thought-provoking installations.
- National Gallery of Victoria (NGV): Australia's oldest and most visited art museum hosts an impressive collection of international and

Australian art. From European masterpieces to cutting-edge contemporary exhibitions, it's a must-visit for art enthusiasts.
- ACMI (Australian Centre for the Moving Image): Located in Federation Square, ACMI explores the world of film, television, and digital culture through interactive exhibits and screenings.

Theatre and Live Performances
Victoria boasts a thriving performing arts scene, with options ranging from Broadway-style musicals to local productions.
- The Melbourne Theatre Company: Catch a high-quality production of classic or contemporary plays at one of Australia's leading theatre companies.
- The Arts Centre Melbourne: This cultural landmark hosts concerts, ballets, and opera performances, offering something for every taste.
- Comedy Festival: The annual Melbourne International Comedy Festival, one of the largest in the world, attracts comedians and audiences from across the globe.

Cultural Festivals
Victoria's calendar is packed with festivals celebrating its diverse culture and creativity:
- Melbourne International Arts Festival: A highlight of the cultural calendar, this festival showcases

innovative performances, installations, and art from around the world.
- White Night: This nighttime celebration transforms Melbourne's streets and buildings into a canvas for light projections, live music, and pop-up performances.
- Melbourne Fringe Festival: Celebrating independent art, this festival offers avant-garde theatre, dance, and multimedia experiences.

Regional Arts and Culture
Victoria's cultural richness extends beyond Melbourne to its charming regional towns.
- Bendigo and Ballarat: These historic gold-rush towns feature impressive galleries such as the Bendigo Art Gallery and the Art Gallery of Ballarat, showcasing both historical and contemporary works.
- Silo Art Trail: This unique experience takes visitors through regional Victoria to see towering grain silos transformed into stunning murals by local and international artists.
- Castlemaine State Festival: Held biennially, this festival brings music, visual arts, and theatre to the picturesque town of Castlemaine.

Indigenous Culture and Heritage

Victoria is home to a rich Indigenous culture that visitors can explore through art, storytelling, and guided experiences.
- Bunjilaka Aboriginal Cultural Centre: Located within the Melbourne Museum, this space highlights Indigenous stories, art, and traditions.
- Brambuk Cultural Centre: In the Grampians (Gariwerd) National Park, this center offers insights into the traditions, stories, and art of the local Djab Wurrung and Jardwadjali peoples.
- Aboriginal Heritage Walk: Take a guided tour through Melbourne's Royal Botanic Gardens to learn about the Indigenous history and culture of the area.

Music and Film Festivals
Victoria's music and film scene thrives with world-class festivals that attract visitors and artists alike.
- Meredith Music Festival: Held in regional Victoria, this multi-day festival blends indie music, camping, and a laid-back atmosphere.
- St Kilda Film Festival: Celebrating Australian short films, this festival is a must for cinephiles.
- Falls Festival: A popular New Year's music festival that features an impressive lineup of international and local artists, set against scenic backdrops.

Fashion and Design

Victoria's flair for style and innovation is evident in its design-focused events.
- Fashion Week: This annual event showcases cutting-edge designs and the city's influence on the global fashion scene.
- Design Week: Explore exhibitions, talks, and workshops that highlight Melbourne's role as a UNESCO City of Design.

Culinary Arts and Food Festivals

Food is art in Victoria, and its culinary festivals celebrate the creativity and passion of chefs and producers.
- Melbourne Food and Wine Festival: A celebration of Victoria's rich food culture, featuring wine tastings, cooking classes, and pop-up dining experiences.
- Grampians Grape Escape: This regional festival combines gourmet food, wine, and live music in a stunning natural setting.

Adventurous Art Experiences

For those looking to combine art with adventure:
- Lightscape at the Royal Botanic Gardens: A nighttime art installation that illuminates the gardens with stunning light displays.
- Outdoor Sculpture Trails: Explore art in nature at locations like the McClelland Sculpture Park or Point Leo Estate.

Victoria's art, culture, and festivals offer a unique blend of adventure and creativity, providing visitors with countless opportunities to immerse themselves in the state's rich cultural tapestry. Whether you're wandering through a bustling city laneway or attending a lively regional festival, you'll find inspiration at every turn.

Family-friendly Activities

Victoria offers a treasure trove of family-friendly activities, making it a perfect destination for visitors traveling with children. From interactive museums and wildlife encounters to outdoor adventures and unique attractions, families will find endless ways to create unforgettable memories together.

Wildlife Encounters

Victoria is home to a variety of wildlife parks and sanctuaries where kids and adults can get up close to Australia's unique animals.

- Melbourne Zoo: Meet iconic Australian species like kangaroos, koalas, and wombats, as well as exotic animals from around the world. The "Growing Wild" area is specially designed for young children.

- Healesville Sanctuary: Located in the Yarra Valley, this sanctuary focuses on native wildlife, offering opportunities to interact with kangaroos and see platypuses in their natural habitats.

- Phillip Island Nature Parks: Witness the famous Penguin Parade, explore the Koala Conservation Reserve, and enjoy a family day at the Nobbies Centre, learning about marine life.

Museums and Interactive Exhibits

Victoria's museums cater to curious young minds with hands-on exhibits and family-friendly programs.

- Scienceworks: Located in Spotswood, this museum is a hit with kids, offering interactive exhibits, a planetarium, and live science demonstrations.
- Melbourne Museum: Home to the Pauline Gandel Children's Gallery, a space for young children to explore, play, and learn through interactive displays.
- Australian Centre for the Moving Image (ACMI): Discover the magic of film, television, and video games through engaging exhibitions and workshops.

Theme Parks and Adventure Activities

For families seeking thrills and excitement, Victoria's theme parks and adventure destinations deliver plenty of fun.

- Luna Park Melbourne: This historic amusement park in St Kilda offers classic rides like the Scenic Railway roller coaster, carnival games, and a whimsical atmosphere.
- Gumbuya World: Located near Melbourne, this park combines wildlife experiences, water slides, and adventure rides for a full day of family entertainment.
- Tree Surfing at Enchanted Adventure Garden: Located on the Mornington Peninsula, this activity combines ziplining, obstacle courses, and giant mazes for adventurous families.

Outdoor Adventures and Natural Wonders
Victoria's great outdoors is a giant playground for families to explore together.
- Great Ocean Road: Take a family road trip to see the Twelve Apostles, stop at kid-friendly beaches, and enjoy scenic picnics along the way.
- Dandenong Ranges: Hop aboard the Puffing Billy Railway, a heritage steam train that winds through the lush forests and hills, or explore the enchanting William Ricketts Sanctuary.
- Wilson's Promontory: Enjoy easy hiking trails, such as the Lilly Pilly Gully walk, or spend the day at family-friendly beaches like Norman Bay.

Farm Visits and Outdoor Play

Introduce children to Victoria's rural charm with visits to working farms and outdoor attractions.
- Collingwood Children's Farm: Located in Melbourne, this urban farm lets kids feed animals, collect eggs, and enjoy the farmers' market.
- Cherry Picking in the Yarra Valley: Seasonal activities like fruit picking allow families to enjoy fresh produce straight from the orchard.
- The Big Goose: Located on the Mornington Peninsula, this farm offers animal feeding, pony rides, and an adventure playground.

Cultural and Creative Activities
Victoria encourages creativity and cultural exploration for young and old alike.
- ArtPlay in Melbourne: Located near Federation Square, this creative hub offers workshops and activities for children to explore art, music, and drama.
- Royal Botanic Gardens: Families can explore the Ian Potter Children's Garden, a fun and educational space for kids to discover plants and nature.
- Festivals: Events like Moomba Festival in Melbourne feature parades, rides, and free family entertainment.

Beaches and Coastal Fun
Victoria's beaches are perfect for families seeking relaxation and seaside adventures.

- St Kilda Beach: Build sandcastles, splash in the calm waters, or take a ride on the seaside carousel.
- Mornington Peninsula: Visit family-friendly beaches like Mount Martha or Rye, which offer shallow waters and safe swimming conditions.
- Anglesea Beach: A great spot for learning to surf, with several surf schools catering to children and beginners.

Family Cycling and Walking Trails
Explore Victoria on two wheels or on foot with these family-friendly trails:
- Merri Creek Trail: A gentle path in Melbourne that's great for walking or biking with kids.
- Warburton Rail Trail: A scenic cycling route that passes through picturesque countryside, suitable for all skill levels.
- Botanic Gardens Walks: Stroll through Melbourne's Royal Botanic Gardens, where kids can spot ducks, enjoy open lawns, and visit the playground.

Aquatic Adventures
Victoria offers plenty of water-based fun for families:
- SEA LIFE Melbourne Aquarium: Marvel at sharks, stingrays, and penguins in this immersive underwater world.

- Splash Parks: Cool off at water play areas like Riverwalk Water Park or the adventure playgrounds scattered throughout Melbourne's suburbs.
- Kayaking in Lake Eildon: A calm and family-friendly spot to paddle and explore the surrounding nature.

Victoria's blend of urban attractions, outdoor adventures, and cultural experiences ensures that families of all ages will find endless opportunities to bond and explore. From petting kangaroos to riding roller coasters, there's something for every child and parent to enjoy in this vibrant state.

Chapter 8

STAYING SAFE AND GREEN

Travel Safety Tips

Victoria is a welcoming and safe destination for travelers, but like any trip, planning and awareness are essential for a smooth and secure experience. Here are some specific tips to help you stay safe during your visit.

Be Prepared for Changing Weather
Victoria's climate can be unpredictable, with sunny mornings turning into rainy afternoons, especially in Melbourne. Pack layers and always carry a lightweight rain jacket or umbrella. Check daily weather forecasts to plan activities accordingly and avoid surprises.

Road Safety

If you're driving, familiarize yourself with Australian road rules. Drive on the left-hand side of the road, and always wear a seatbelt.
- Be cautious on rural roads, especially at dusk or dawn, as wildlife like kangaroos may be crossing.
- Observe speed limits, which can vary between urban, suburban, and highway areas.
- For road trips, ensure your vehicle is in good condition, with a spare tire and emergency kit on board.

Bushfire Awareness

Victoria's summers can bring bushfire risks, especially in rural and forested areas.
- Check the Fire Danger Ratings daily on the VicEmergency website or app.
- Avoid high-risk areas during Total Fire Ban days, and follow all local authority warnings or evacuation orders.
- If camping, always use designated campfire spots and extinguish fires thoroughly.

Sun Protection

Victoria's sun can be strong, even on cooler days. Protect yourself to avoid sunburn or heat-related illnesses.
- Use sunscreen with high SPF, and reapply regularly, especially if swimming or sweating.

- Wear a wide-brimmed hat and sunglasses, and seek shade during the hottest parts of the day (10 a.m. to 4 p.m.).
- Stay hydrated by carrying a reusable water bottle and drinking plenty of water throughout the day.

Swimming and Water Safety
Victoria's beaches and waterways are beautiful but can pose risks if precautions aren't taken.
- Swim only at patrolled beaches and stay between the red and yellow flags where lifeguards are present.
- Be mindful of rip currents; if caught in one, stay calm, float, and raise your hand for help.
- Observe warning signs near rivers, lakes, and waterfalls to avoid unsafe swimming areas or slippery rocks.

Urban Safety
Victoria's cities and towns are generally safe, but it's always wise to stay alert.
- Avoid poorly lit or unfamiliar areas at night, and stick to well-trafficked streets.
- Keep your belongings secure, especially in crowded areas like festivals or markets.
- Be cautious with personal information and avoid sharing travel plans with strangers.

Hiking and Outdoor Safety

Victoria's parks and trails offer incredible experiences, but preparation is key.
- Inform someone of your plans if hiking in remote areas, and stick to marked trails.
- Carry a map, enough water, snacks, and a first-aid kit. A fully charged phone with offline maps can also be helpful.
- Be mindful of wildlife; avoid feeding animals and keep a safe distance.

Health and Medical Preparedness
Health services in Victoria are excellent, but it's important to be prepared for minor issues.
- Purchase travel insurance that covers medical emergencies, including outdoor activities like hiking or water sports.
- Carry any necessary medications and a small travel first-aid kit with bandages, antiseptic, and pain relievers.
- Note the location of the nearest medical facilities or pharmacies in the area you're staying.

Emergency Contacts
Ensure you know how to seek help in an emergency.
- Dial 000 for police, fire, or ambulance assistance in Australia.
- Download the VicEmergency app for real-time alerts and safety information.

- Keep local contact numbers, such as your accommodation or tour operators, handy for immediate assistance.

Cultural Etiquette

Respecting local customs and regulations enhances safety and your overall travel experience.
- Observe rules at cultural sites, including Indigenous areas, and seek permission before taking photographs.
- Adhere to alcohol consumption laws, including restrictions in public areas.
- Dispose of litter responsibly and follow environmental guidelines in natural areas.

By staying informed and prepared, you can enjoy Victoria's diverse offerings with peace of mind, ensuring a safe and memorable journey.

Sustainable Tourism In Victoria

Victoria is not only a stunning destination but also a region deeply committed to preserving its natural beauty and cultural heritage for future generations. Sustainable tourism plays a significant role in ensuring that visitors can enjoy its attractions responsibly, supporting local communities and protecting the environment.

Choosing Eco-Friendly Accommodation
Victoria offers a wide range of eco-conscious lodging options. Look for accommodations with certifications such as EarthCheck, Green Star, or Ecotourism Australia.
- Eco-lodges: These properties often use renewable energy, rainwater harvesting, and sustainable materials. Many are located in pristine areas, like the Grampians or Great Otway National Park.
- Sustainable hotels: In Melbourne and other urban areas, many hotels now prioritize energy-efficient systems, waste reduction programs, and eco-friendly amenities.

Supporting Local Businesses
Sustainable tourism involves uplifting local communities. In Victoria, visitors can support small businesses and artisans:
- Farm-to-table dining: Many restaurants across Victoria source produce from local farmers, offering fresher food while supporting the region's agricultural community.
- Handmade goods and crafts: Visit local markets, like the Queen Victoria Market in Melbourne or regional markets in the Yarra Valley, to purchase unique items made by local artisans.

Reducing Carbon Footprint While Traveling

Victoria has an extensive public transportation network, making it easy to explore sustainably:
- Use trains, trams, and buses instead of private vehicles. Public transit reduces emissions and offers a cost-effective way to explore urban and regional areas.
- For short distances, rent bicycles or walk, especially in cities like Melbourne where bike-friendly paths and pedestrian walkways are common.

Participating in Conservation Activities
Many of Victoria's attractions offer opportunities for visitors to engage in conservation:
- Wildlife sanctuaries: Places like Healesville Sanctuary and Moonlit Sanctuary focus on protecting endangered species and educating visitors about conservation.
- Tree planting and clean-up programs: Some community organizations and eco-tours allow visitors to participate in activities like tree planting or beach clean-ups, contributing directly to environmental preservation.

Eco-Friendly Adventures
Victoria's natural landscapes provide endless eco-friendly activities that leave a minimal environmental impact:

- Hiking: Explore trails in national parks such as Wilsons Promontory, Grampians, or the Dandenong Ranges. Stick to designated paths to protect fragile ecosystems.
- Wildlife watching: Enjoy encounters with animals in their natural habitats, such as penguins at Phillip Island or koalas along the Great Ocean Road. Choose operators that follow ethical wildlife tourism guidelines.
- Sustainable winery tours: The Yarra Valley and Mornington Peninsula offer eco-conscious winery tours that focus on organic and biodynamic winemaking practices.

Practicing Responsible Behavior
Travelers can make a significant difference by adopting simple, sustainable habits:
- Carry reusable items: Bring reusable water bottles, coffee cups, and shopping bags to reduce plastic waste.
- Respect nature: Avoid disturbing wildlife, refrain from picking plants, and follow "leave no trace" principles.
- Recycle and compost: Use recycling bins available at most attractions and accommodations. In rural areas, inquire about composting facilities or waste disposal guidelines.

Exploring Indigenous Tourism

Respecting and learning from Victoria's Indigenous heritage is an essential part of sustainable tourism:
- Participate in tours led by Traditional Owners to gain a deeper understanding of the culture, history, and connection to the land. Experiences like Worn Gundidj tours in the Great Otway National Park provide insights into Indigenous traditions and ecological knowledge.
- Visit sacred sites respectfully, such as the Budj Bim Cultural Landscape, a UNESCO World Heritage Site showcasing ancient aquaculture systems.

Joining Green Initiatives
Victoria promotes several sustainability-focused initiatives for both locals and tourists:
- Plastic-free zones: Many beaches and public areas encourage visitors to avoid single-use plastics.
- EcoFestivals: Events like the Sustainable Living Festival in Melbourne celebrate environmental awareness and inspire sustainable lifestyles.
- Green transport options: Some cities, including Melbourne, offer electric scooters and car-share services, providing low-emission travel alternatives.

Being a Conscious Traveler
Sustainable tourism is not just about the destination but also how you engage with it:

- Travel during off-peak seasons to reduce overcrowding and minimize strain on local resources.
- Limit your energy and water usage at accommodations. Turn off lights, avoid long showers, and reuse towels.
- Share knowledge: Encourage others to adopt sustainable practices by setting a positive example and sharing your eco-friendly travel experiences.

By incorporating these sustainable practices, visitors to Victoria can play an active role in protecting its vibrant landscapes, diverse wildlife, and rich cultural heritage, ensuring that this remarkable region continues to thrive for generations to come.

Chapter 9

SAMPLED ITINERARIES

Iconic Road Trips

Victoria's compact size and diverse landscapes make it ideal for unforgettable road trips. Whether you're drawn to dramatic coastlines, serene mountains, or charming regional towns, these iconic itineraries showcase the best the state has to offer.

The Great Ocean Road Adventure
Duration: 3–5 days
Highlights:
- Torquay: Begin your journey at the surf capital of Australia. Visit Bells Beach and explore the Australian National Surfing Museum.

- Lorne: Enjoy coastal charm with walks to Erskine Falls and a visit to Teddy's Lookout for panoramic views.
- The Twelve Apostles: Witness these iconic limestone stacks at sunrise or sunset for breathtaking views.
- Gibson Steps and Loch Ard Gorge: Marvel at the dramatic cliffs and learn about the area's shipwreck history.
- Warrnambool: Finish your trip at this historic town, where whale-watching is popular during winter.

Yarra Valley Wine and Nature Getaway
Duration: 2–3 days
Highlights:
- Lilydale: Start your trip at the gateway to the Yarra Valley and stop at Yarra Ranges Regional Museum.
- Wineries: Tour world-class vineyards, such as Domaine Chandon and TarraWarra Estate, for tastings and meals.
- Healesville Sanctuary: Encounter Australia's unique wildlife in a stunning bushland setting.
- SkyHigh Mount Dandenong: End your trip with sweeping views over Melbourne and lush gardens to explore.

High Country Alpine Drive

Duration: 4–6 days
Highlights:
- Bright: Stroll through tree-lined streets, sample local food, and enjoy cycling trails.
- Mount Hotham: In winter, this alpine village offers skiing; in summer, it transforms into a hiker's paradise.
- Falls Creek: Another ski destination that boasts scenic trails and mountain biking during warmer months.
- Beechworth: Dive into history with well-preserved gold rush-era architecture and local produce, especially honey.

The Murray River Road
Duration: 4–5 days
Highlights:
- Echuca: Discover paddle steamers and learn about the historic port.
- Swan Hill: Visit the Pioneer Settlement and experience life as it was during the 19th century.
- Mildura: Explore this riverside city with its thriving arts scene, nearby wineries, and fresh local produce.
- Lake Boga Flying Boat Museum: Learn about the region's wartime history.

Phillip Island and Bass Coast
Duration: 2–3 days

Highlights:
- San Remo: Start your journey at this charming coastal town, and watch pelican feeding at the jetty.
- Phillip Island: Witness the iconic Penguin Parade, explore the Koala Conservation Reserve, and visit the Nobbies Centre for stunning ocean views.
- Churchill Island Heritage Farm: Learn about Victoria's farming history and enjoy hands-on activities.
- Kilcunda Coastal Trail: Walk along rugged cliffs with breathtaking views of the Southern Ocean.

Goldfields Heritage Trail
Duration: 3–4 days
Highlights:
- Ballarat: Explore Sovereign Hill, an open-air museum that brings the gold rush era to life.
- Bendigo: Discover the city's rich history with a visit to the Central Deborah Gold Mine and the Bendigo Art Gallery.
- Castlemaine: Enjoy vibrant cafes, vintage shops, and historical landmarks.
- Maldon: A quaint town known for its preserved 19th-century charm, ideal for photography and heritage tours.

Gippsland Lakes Coastal Drive
Duration: 3–5 days
Highlights:

- Wilson's Promontory: Hike the trails, enjoy wildlife spotting, and relax on pristine beaches.
- Lakes Entrance: Explore Australia's largest network of inland waterways by boat or kayak.
- Metung and Paynesville: Visit charming waterside villages and enjoy fresh seafood.
- Ninety Mile Beach: Experience the serenity of this unspoiled stretch of sand and sea.

Grampians Nature Escape
Duration: 3–4 days
Highlights:
- Halls Gap: Start your journey at this charming town in the heart of the Grampians National Park.
- Mackenzie Falls: Marvel at the cascading water on one of the park's most iconic walks.
- Pinnacle Lookout: Hike to this vantage point for panoramic views of the rugged landscape.
- Aboriginal Rock Art Sites: Learn about Indigenous heritage at sites like Gulgurn Manja and Bunjil's Shelter.

Mornington Peninsula Retreat
Duration: 2–3 days
Highlights:
- Peninsula Hot Springs: Relax in natural thermal pools surrounded by serene landscapes.

- Sorrento and Portsea: Discover historic towns with boutique shopping, coastal walks, and stunning views.
- Cape Schanck Lighthouse: Explore dramatic cliffs and trails around this historic site.
- Red Hill: Visit wineries and farm gates to sample the region's best produce.

Outer Melbourne Day Trip Highlights
For those short on time, several day trips from Melbourne offer incredible experiences:
- Dandenong Ranges: Enjoy lush forests, charming villages, and the Puffing Billy steam train.
- Macedon Ranges: Visit Hanging Rock, explore gardens, and indulge in gourmet food.
- Daylesford and Hepburn Springs: Relax in mineral spas and discover local art galleries.

Each road trip offers a unique perspective on Victoria's beauty, history, and culture. With careful planning and an adventurous spirit, you'll uncover countless gems along the way.

Weekend Escapes
Victoria offers a range of short, yet enriching weekend getaway options. Whether you're seeking nature, culture, or coastal relaxation, these weekend

escapes let you experience the best of what the state has to offer in just a few days.

1. Yarra Valley and Dandenong Ranges Escape
Duration: 2 Days
Highlights:
- Day 1:
  - Morning: Start your day with a scenic drive to the Yarra Valley, about 1 hour from Melbourne. Head to a few renowned wineries such as Domaine Chandon and Yering Station for tastings and lunch with stunning vineyard views.
  - Afternoon: Visit the Healesville Sanctuary, where you can see koalas, kangaroos, and a variety of native Australian animals in a natural setting.
  - Evening: Stay at a cozy vineyard accommodation or eco-lodge in the Yarra Valley for a relaxing night surrounded by nature.
- Day 2:
  - Morning: Drive to the Dandenong Ranges, about 1 hour south of Melbourne. Take a ride on the iconic Puffing Billy Railway, a heritage steam train offering beautiful views of the lush landscape.
  - Afternoon: Explore the National Rhododendron Gardens or walk through the towering trees at the Sherbrooke Forest.
  - Evening: Enjoy dinner at a local café or winery before heading back to Melbourne.

2. Great Ocean Road Short Break

Duration: 2 Days

Highlights:

- Day 1:

  - Morning: Start early for the scenic Great Ocean Road drive. Stop at Torquay, the surf capital, and visit Bells Beach. Continue towards Lorne, a beautiful coastal town, and stop for lunch by the beach.

  - Afternoon: Explore the Erskine Falls and take a walk through the Great Otway National Park to discover lush forests and tranquil waterfalls.

  - Evening: Stay at one of Lorne's charming boutique accommodations and enjoy a seaside dinner.

- Day 2:

  - Morning: Drive to the Twelve Apostles and marvel at these towering limestone stacks at sunrise or early morning for the best lighting.

  - Late Morning: Visit Loch Ard Gorge, learn about the shipwreck history, and take a walk along the cliffs.

  - Afternoon: Head towards Port Campbell for a relaxed lunch, then make your way back to Melbourne via Colac.

3. Mornington Peninsula Coastal Retreat

Duration: 2 Days

Highlights:

- Day 1:
- Morning: Drive about 1.5 hours south from Melbourne to the Mornington Peninsula. Start with a visit to Peninsula Hot Springs, where you can relax in natural thermal pools surrounded by rolling hills.
- Afternoon: Visit Sorrento for boutique shopping and lunch by the water. Afterward, take a coastal walk along Point Nepean National Park, exploring historic sites and enjoying stunning views of Bass Strait.
- Evening: Enjoy a waterfront dinner at a local restaurant and stay in one of the region's charming bed-and-breakfast accommodations.
- Day 2:
- Morning: Explore the coastal town of Portsea and take a walk along the cliff-top trails or enjoy some beach time.
- Afternoon: Visit the iconic Cape Schanck Lighthouse and enjoy panoramic views of the ocean.
- Late Afternoon: Take a detour to Red Hill for a wine tasting at one of its boutique wineries before heading back to Melbourne.

4. Phillip Island Wildlife and Coastal Adventure
Duration: 2 Days
Highlights:
- Day 1:

- Morning: Drive to Phillip Island, about 2 hours from Melbourne. Begin with a visit to the Koala Conservation Centre to spot koalas up close in their natural habitat.

  - Afternoon: Explore Churchill Island, known for its heritage farm and stunning coastal views. Afterward, head to Cowes for a casual seaside lunch and some beach time.

  - Evening: Watch the Penguin Parade at Phillip Island Nature Parks as the little penguins return to their burrows at sunset. Stay overnight in Cowes or a nearby beachfront accommodation.

- Day 2:

  - Morning: Visit the Nobbies Centre to walk along boardwalks and observe seals in the wild.

  - Afternoon: Spend the afternoon exploring the island's sandy beaches and coastal trails. Head back to Melbourne by the evening, with a stop at San Remo for a relaxed lunch by the beach.

5. Grampians National Park Nature Escape
Duration: 2 Days
Highlights:
- Day 1:

  - Morning: Depart from Melbourne and head to the Grampians National Park, about 3 hours away. Stop in Halls Gap for a quick break, then check into your accommodation.

- Afternoon: Explore the Mackenzie Falls, one of the largest and most stunning waterfalls in the region.
- Evening: Enjoy a relaxed dinner in Halls Gap with local produce, such as venison or trout, and settle into a lodge or cabin.

- Day 2:
- Morning: Hike the Pinnacle Lookout for panoramic views of the rugged mountains and valleys below.
- Late Morning: Visit the Aboriginal Rock Art sites in the area to learn about the region's Indigenous history.
- Afternoon: Take a scenic drive through the park, spotting wildlife such as kangaroos, emus, and wallabies before heading back to Melbourne.

6. Daylesford and Hepburn Springs Wellness Getaway
Duration: 2 Days
Highlights:
- Day 1:
- Morning: Head to Daylesford, about 1.5 hours from Melbourne. Start your visit with a relaxing soak at the Hepburn Bathhouse & Spa, known for its mineral-rich waters.
- Afternoon: Explore the local markets for fresh produce, gourmet food, and arts and crafts. Take a

leisurely stroll around Lake Daylesford or enjoy a coffee at one of the charming local cafes.

- Evening: Enjoy dinner at one of the region's farm-to-table restaurants and stay overnight in a quaint B&B or boutique hotel.

- Day 2:

- Morning: Visit the Lavandula Swiss Italian Farm, where you can wander through fields of lavender and enjoy a coffee at the farm café.

- Afternoon: Continue to Mount Franklin for a scenic walk and enjoy panoramic views of the surrounding landscape before heading back to Melbourne.

These weekend escapes provide an ideal blend of relaxation, adventure, and nature, making them perfect for a short getaway to recharge while discovering the diverse beauty of Victoria.

Comprehensive City And Regional Tours

Victoria is home to vibrant cities, charming regional towns, and breathtaking natural landscapes. These thoughtfully designed city and regional tour itineraries allow you to immerse yourself in the best the state has to offer, combining urban exploration with outdoor adventures and cultural experiences.

1. Melbourne City Exploration

Duration: 2–3 Days

Highlights:

- Day 1:

- Morning: Start your day with a visit to Federation Square, a cultural hub in the heart of Melbourne. Explore the National Gallery of Victoria (NGV) and the Australian Centre for Contemporary Art (ACCA).

- Afternoon: Take a stroll through Laneways and Arcades such as Hosier Lane, known for street art, and Block Arcade for boutique shopping. Enjoy lunch at one of the cafes in Degraves Street or Centre Place.

- Evening: Head to Eureka Skydeck for stunning views of the city skyline at sunset. For dinner, indulge in world-class dining at Chin Chin or Attica.

- Day 2:

- Morning: Explore Royal Botanic Gardens and enjoy a peaceful boat ride on Lake Melbourne.

- Afternoon: Visit Queen Victoria Market, where you can shop for local produce, artisan goods, and specialty items. Then, make your way to Melbourne Museum for an educational experience showcasing Australia's history and culture.

- Evening: Check out Melbourne's vibrant dining scene in Fitzroy or Collingwood, known for their hip restaurants and bars.

- Day 3 (Optional):

- Morning: Take a half-day trip to St Kilda to enjoy the beach, explore Luna Park, or visit the St Kilda Pier.

- Afternoon: If you have extra time, visit Brighton Beach and take in the colorful bathing boxes before returning to the city.

2. Great Ocean Road and Western Victoria Regional Tour

Duration: 3–4 Days

Highlights:

- Day 1:

- Morning: Begin your adventure by heading west along the Great Ocean Road from Melbourne. Stop at Torquay for a surf lesson or beach walk, then continue to Anglesea for scenic views.

- Afternoon: Reach Lorne for lunch by the beach, then hike to Erskine Falls or take a scenic drive to Teddy's Lookout.

- Evening: Stay in Lorne for the night, enjoying fresh seafood for dinner at one of the town's waterfront restaurants.

- Day 2:

- Morning: Travel towards the Twelve Apostles and stop at Loch Ard Gorge to learn about shipwreck history and take a short walk.

- Afternoon: Explore Port Campbell National Park for other stunning natural features, then head to Warrnambool.

- Evening: Stay in Warrnambool and enjoy a visit to Logan's Beach for whale watching during the winter months.

- Day 3:

 - Morning: Visit the Tower Hill Wildlife Reserve near Warrnambool to spot native animals like emus and koalas.

 - Afternoon: Head north to Port Fairy, a historic town known for its well-preserved 19th-century cottages and great food.

 - Evening: Stay overnight in Port Fairy or continue your journey back to Melbourne.

3. Grampians National Park and High Country Tour

Duration: 3–4 Days

Highlights:

- Day 1:

 - Morning: Depart Melbourne early and head to Halls Gap, the gateway to Grampians National Park.

 - Afternoon: Hike to Mackenzie Falls, one of the most iconic waterfalls in the region, or take the Grampians Peaks Trail for a more challenging trek.

 - Evening: Stay in Halls Gap in a cozy lodge or cabin surrounded by nature.

- Day 2:

- Morning: Explore Pinnacle Lookout for panoramic views of the Grampians' rugged mountains and valleys.
- Afternoon: Take a scenic drive to Aboriginal Rock Art Sites in the park, such as Bunjil's Shelter and Gulgurn Manja.
- Evening: Have a relaxed dinner at one of the local restaurants in Halls Gap.

- Day 3:
- Morning: Drive towards Bright in the Alpine Region, passing through Beechworth, a historic gold rush town.
- Afternoon: Stop for lunch in Bright, and spend the afternoon exploring the town's charming streets and outdoor activities, including cycling or visiting Mount Buffalo National Park.
- Evening: Stay in Bright, known for its boutique accommodations and farm-to-table dining options.

- Day 4 (Optional):
- Morning: Take a scenic drive to Mount Hotham for a mountain retreat, either for skiing in winter or hiking in summer.
- Afternoon: Visit Falls Creek, another alpine village, before returning to Melbourne.

4. Phillip Island and Gippsland Regional Tour
Duration: 2–3 Days
Highlights:
- Day 1:

- Morning: Head south from Melbourne to Phillip Island. Begin with a visit to Koala Conservation Centre to see native wildlife.

- Afternoon: Spend the afternoon at Churchill Island Heritage Farm, where you can engage in activities like feeding animals and watching demonstrations.

- Evening: Watch the famous Penguin Parade at Phillip Island Nature Parks as little penguins return to their burrows at dusk. Stay overnight in Cowes.

- Day 2:

- Morning: Explore the rugged coastline of Cape Woolamai, where you can take walks along pristine beaches and enjoy breathtaking views.

- Afternoon: Drive through the Gippsland region, stopping at charming towns like Sale or Maffra for lunch.

- Evening: Enjoy a meal at a local pub or restaurant before heading to Lakes Entrance for the night.

- Day 3:

- Morning: Explore Lakes Entrance's natural beauty, including boat tours of the Gippsland Lakes.

- Afternoon: Head towards Wilson's Promontory, a nature-lover's haven with stunning beaches, hiking trails, and wildlife.

- Evening: Return to Melbourne, or stay overnight at Tidal River to enjoy more time in the wilderness.

5. Murray River and Goldfields Regional Tour
Duration: 3 Days
Highlights:
- Day 1:
  - Morning: Start your journey at Echuca, an iconic town on the Murray River. Take a cruise on a historic paddle steamer and explore the Port of Echuca.
  - Afternoon: Head to Swan Hill, where you can visit the Pioneer Settlement and discover the area's rich history.
  - Evening: Stay in Mildura, known for its arts and food scene, and enjoy a riverside dinner.
- Day 2:
  - Morning: Visit the Mildura Arts Centre or Chaffey Trail for a day of culture and history.
  - Afternoon: Explore the Murray-Sunset National Park, known for its vast saltbush plains and unique landscape.
  - Evening: Stay overnight in Mildura, known for its wineries and local produce.
- Day 3:
  - Morning: Head south to Bendigo, a historic gold rush town with beautiful architecture.
  - Afternoon: Explore Bendigo Art Gallery and Central Deborah Gold Mine.
  - Evening: Return to Melbourne after a fulfilling day of exploration.

These comprehensive city and regional tour itineraries offer a mix of cultural exploration, outdoor adventures, and picturesque landscapes, ensuring that you make the most of your time in Victoria. Whether you're in the mood for city life, coastal adventures, or historic towns, Victoria has something for every traveler.

Chapter 10

NOTABLE SITES AND TOP TOURIST SPOTS

Melbourne Highlights

Melbourne, the cultural capital of Australia, offers a diverse range of attractions that appeal to history buffs, art lovers, nature enthusiasts, and foodies alike. From its vibrant laneways and hidden cafes to iconic landmarks and beautiful gardens, Melbourne is a city that promises something for everyone. Here are some of the top highlights and must-see tourist spots in Melbourne:

1. Federation Square
Located at the heart of the city, Federation Square is a modern architectural masterpiece that serves as a

cultural precinct. It is home to several key attractions, including the Australian Centre for the Moving Image (ACMI), the National Gallery of Victoria (NGV), and various galleries, restaurants, and cafes. Federation Square is also known for hosting numerous events, festivals, and live performances throughout the year.

2. Royal Botanic Gardens

The Royal Botanic Gardens is an oasis of greenery in the middle of the city. With sprawling lawns, tranquil lakes, and over 8,000 plant species, it's an ideal spot for a leisurely walk or picnic. Highlights include the Tan Track, which is a popular jogging route, and the Kereek Walk, where you can explore native Australian plants. The gardens are a perfect place to relax and immerse yourself in nature.

3. Eureka Skydeck

For a stunning bird's-eye view of Melbourne, the Eureka Skydeck is a must-visit. Located on the 88th floor of the Eureka Tower, it offers 360-degree views of the city skyline, the Yarra River, and beyond. For an added thrill, try the Edge Experience, a glass cube that extends out from the building, giving you a unique view of the city beneath your feet.

4. Melbourne Museum and Royal Exhibition Building

Melbourne's history and culture come alive at the Melbourne Museum, which offers exhibits ranging from the ancient to the contemporary. The Royal Exhibition Building, located in the museum precinct, is a UNESCO World Heritage site and an architectural gem. It is often used for events and exhibitions and offers a glimpse into Melbourne's rich past.

5. Queen Victoria Market

A trip to Melbourne wouldn't be complete without visiting the Queen Victoria Market, one of the largest open-air markets in the Southern Hemisphere. This bustling market offers a wide range of fresh produce, gourmet food, and artisanal goods. It's the perfect place to sample local delicacies, shop for souvenirs, or experience Melbourne's multicultural atmosphere.

6. Hosier Lane

For a taste of Melbourne's vibrant street art scene, head to Hosier Lane, one of the city's most iconic laneways. It is constantly evolving with new murals and graffiti art, making it a living canvas that attracts photographers and art lovers. The lane also has several hidden bars and cafes, making it a popular spot to grab a coffee or cocktail while soaking in the creative energy.

7. *Flinders Street Station*
Flinders Street Station is Melbourne's most iconic train station and a significant landmark. Known for its grand yellow façade and the large clock on its front, the station is a major transportation hub and a great starting point for exploring the city. The Flinders Street Viaduct is also a great spot for photos, offering a view of the city's skyline.

8. *St Kilda Beach*
If you're looking for a beach day, St Kilda Beach is Melbourne's most popular coastal destination. Just a short tram ride from the city center, St Kilda offers a lively atmosphere, with its famous St Kilda Pier, the iconic Luna Park, and plenty of cafes, restaurants, and bars. It's a great place to relax, enjoy a swim, or take a sunset stroll along the beach.

9. *National Gallery of Victoria (NGV)*
As Australia's oldest and most visited public art museum, the National Gallery of Victoria (NGV) is a must-see for art lovers. It boasts a stunning collection of international and Australian art, including European paintings, Asian art, decorative arts, and contemporary works. The museum is

housed in two main buildings: the NGV International on St Kilda Road and the Ian Potter Centre in Federation Square.

10. *Melbourne Zoo*

The Melbourne Zoo, located just a short distance from the city center, is home to over 300 species of animals from around the world. It's a great spot for families and animal lovers, with exhibits showcasing everything from native Australian wildlife to exotic creatures. The Gorilla Rainforest and **Wild Sea** sections are particularly popular for their immersive animal experiences.

These highlights represent just a small taste of what Melbourne has to offer. Whether you're exploring its cultural sites, iconic landmarks, or hidden gems, Melbourne is a city that never ceases to surprise and inspire.

Great Ocean Road And Twelve Apostles

The Great Ocean Road is one of the most scenic coastal drives in the world, stretching over 240 kilometers along the southern coast of Victoria. Known for its stunning views, rugged cliffs, charming seaside towns, and natural wonders, the Great Ocean Road is a must-see for any visitor to Victoria. Among the many incredible stops along the way, the Twelve Apostles is one of the most iconic and awe-inspiring landmarks.

Great Ocean Road
The Great Ocean Road is more than just a scenic route; it's an adventure in itself. The drive begins just outside Melbourne and winds its way along the coastline, offering breathtaking views of the Southern Ocean, lush rainforests, and rugged cliffs. The road is dotted with picturesque towns, including Torquay, the surfing capital of Australia,

Anglesea, Lorne, and Apollo Bay, each with its own charm and attractions.

- Torquay: Known as the birthplace of Australian surfing, Torquay is a haven for surf enthusiasts. Visitors can enjoy the beautiful beaches, surf lessons, and explore the Australian National Surfing Museum.

- Lorne: A coastal town with a mix of natural beauty and local history, Lorne is famous for its Erskine Falls, tranquil beaches, and vibrant food scene. It's a great place to relax and enjoy the ocean air.

- Apollo Bay: A perfect spot to stop for lunch or an overnight stay, Apollo Bay offers stunning coastal views, and from here, visitors can explore the Great Otway National Park, home to lush rainforests and waterfalls.

The drive along the Great Ocean Road is a photographer's paradise, with numerous lookout points where you can stop and take in the sweeping views of the ocean, cliffs, and beaches.

Twelve Apostles
The Twelve Apostles are perhaps the most famous and photographed natural feature along the Great

Ocean Road. Located in the Campbell National Park, these towering limestone stacks rise majestically from the Southern Ocean. Formed by millions of years of erosion, the Twelve Apostles are a striking reminder of the power of nature. Originally, there were twelve limestone pillars, but due to erosion, only eight remain today.

Visitors can view the Twelve Apostles from a series of well-placed viewing platforms, which offer dramatic views of the formations set against the backdrop of the ocean and sky. The best time to visit is at sunrise or sunset when the colors of the sky and the sea create a magical atmosphere. The Twelve Apostles are a must-see for anyone traveling along the Great Ocean Road and a perfect spot for photography.

Beyond the Twelve Apostles, visitors can explore other nearby attractions, such as:

- Loch Ard Gorge: A short drive from the Twelve Apostles, this beautiful inlet is named after the shipwreck of the Loch Ard in 1878. The gorge features stunning cliffs, beaches, and walking trails that tell the story of the shipwreck.
- The Arch: A natural rock formation created by years of erosion, the Arch is another stunning

coastal feature just a short drive from the Twelve Apostles.
- The Grotto: A picturesque limestone sinkhole with an opening to the sea, this site offers a unique perspective on the region's geology.

Whether you're driving the Great Ocean Road in its entirety or just visiting the Twelve Apostles, these landmarks are an unforgettable experience. The dramatic coastline, rich history, and natural beauty make the Great Ocean Road and the Twelve Apostles a top destination for anyone exploring Victoria.

Phillip Island And Wildlife Parks

Phillip Island is one of Victoria's most beloved destinations, renowned for its natural beauty, wildlife experiences, and laid-back atmosphere. Located just a 90-minute drive from Melbourne, the island offers visitors a unique blend of coastal landscapes, wildlife encounters, and family-friendly activities. The island is best known for its famous Penguin Parade, but it also offers numerous other attractions and natural wonders, making it a must-visit destination in Victoria.

Phillip Island Penguin Parade
The Penguin Parade is one of Australia's most iconic wildlife experiences. Every evening, visitors can watch as hundreds of Little Penguins (the world's smallest penguin species) waddle up the beach to their burrows after a day of fishing. The event takes place at Summerland Beach, where the penguins return to shore at sunset. The Phillip Island Penguin Parade is a must-see, and the experience can be enhanced with various viewing options, including boardwalks and enclosed viewing areas, offering unobstructed views of the penguins' fascinating journey.

Phillip Island is also home to a Penguin Parade Visitor Centre, which provides informative exhibits and interactive displays about the penguins, their behavior, and the conservation efforts aimed at protecting them.

Koala Conservation Centre

For those interested in Australia's iconic wildlife, the Koala Conservation Centreon Phillip Island offers a unique opportunity to observe koalas in their natural habitat. The centre features a network of elevated boardwalks that allow visitors to get up close to the koalas without disturbing them. The centre is set in a tranquil eucalyptus forest, and visitors can often spot koalas lounging in the trees, as well as various bird species and other native animals.

Educational displays at the Koala Conservation Centre explain the koalas' role in the ecosystem, their conservation challenges, and the ongoing efforts to protect their populations.

Phillip Island Nature Parks
Phillip Island is home to a range of protected areas that showcase the island's rich natural heritage. The Phillip Island Nature Parks encompasses several conservation areas, including the Koala Conservation Centre, The Nobbies, and Churchill Island Heritage Farm, each offering a distinct experience.

- The Nobbies: Located at the western tip of Phillip Island, The Nobbies is a spectacular coastal area featuring rugged cliffs, blowholes, and views over the Bass Strait. The Nobbies Centre provides visitors with information about the region's history, geology, and wildlife, and offers panoramic views of the coastline and nearby Seal Rocks, home to Australia's largest fur seal colony.

- Churchill Island Heritage Farm: This historic working farm allows visitors to step back in time and experience life on an early Australian farm. Visitors can interact with heritage farm animals, explore the gardens, and watch traditional farming demonstrations. The farm is also a great place to enjoy scenic views of the island's coastline.

Phillip Island Wildlife Park
The Phillip Island Wildlife Park is another top attraction for those wanting to interact with Australia's unique animals. Set on 60 acres of natural bushland, the wildlife park is home to a wide variety of native species, including kangaroos, wallabies, emus, koalas, and many bird species. The park allows visitors to walk freely among the animals, offering an immersive experience where you can feed kangaroos and wallabies, pet koalas, and learn about Australia's diverse wildlife. The park is family-friendly and a great option for those traveling with children.

Phillip Island Beaches and Scenic Views

Aside from its wildlife attractions, Phillip Island also offers some stunning beaches, perfect for swimming, surfing, or relaxing by the sea. Smiths Beach and Cape Woolamai Beach are popular with surfers, while Cowes Beach is known for its calm waters, making it ideal for families and swimmers. The island is also home to many walking trails that offer spectacular views of the coastline, cliffs, and wildlife, making it a great destination for nature lovers and outdoor enthusiasts.

Phillip Island Chocolate Factory
For a sweet treat after a day of wildlife watching, head to the Phillip Island Chocolate Factory, located near the entrance to the island. Here, visitors can enjoy interactive chocolate-making displays, indulge in a variety of locally made chocolates, and even take part in chocolate-making workshops. It's a fun stop for all ages, especially those with a sweet tooth.

Rhyll Inlet and Conservation Reserves
For nature lovers and birdwatchers, Rhyll Inlet is a scenic spot located on the northern part of Phillip Island. The inlet is home to a wide variety of bird species, including migratory shorebirds, making it a popular destination for birdwatching and photography. The Rhyll Inlet Conservation Reserve offers walking trails and viewing platforms,

providing excellent opportunities to explore the region's wetlands and coastal ecosystems.

Bass Strait and Scenic Drives
Exploring Phillip Island by car is a rewarding experience, with numerous scenic drives around the island that offer spectacular views of the coastline, bays, and cliffs. A drive along The Island's Coastal Drive will take you past rugged cliffs, hidden beaches, and small villages, making it the perfect way to experience the natural beauty of the island at your own pace.

Phillip Island is truly a haven for nature and wildlife lovers, offering an unforgettable experience that combines natural beauty with unique wildlife encounters. From the iconic Penguin Parade to koala conservation and family-friendly wildlife parks, Phillip Island is a top destination for those exploring Victoria.

Yarra Valley And Dandenong Ranges

The Yarra Valley and Dandenong Ranges are two of Victoria's most beloved and accessible natural destinations, offering visitors a mix of stunning landscapes, world-class wine regions, charming villages, and abundant outdoor activities. Just a short drive from Melbourne, these regions are perfect for a day trip or a weekend escape, providing a peaceful retreat from the hustle and bustle of the city.

Yarra Valley
The Yarra Valley is renowned for its picturesque vineyards, rolling hills, and lush countryside, making it a premier destination for wine lovers and nature enthusiasts alike. The valley is Victoria's most famous wine-producing region, with a history of over 150 years in winemaking, and it's home to some of Australia's finest wineries and vineyards.

- Wine Tasting and Vineyards: The Yarra Valley boasts over 80 wineries, producing premium cool-climate wines, including Pinot Noir, Chardonnay, and sparkling wines. Visitors can explore Domaine Chandon, Yering Station, Rochford Wines, and Healesville Sanctuary for wine tastings, gourmet food pairings, and stunning vineyard views. Many wineries also offer cellar-door experiences, where guests can sample local wines and enjoy lunch at winery restaurants that highlight fresh, regional produce.

- Healesville Sanctuary: Located in the heart of the Yarra Valley, Healesville Sanctuary offers an opportunity to encounter Australia's most iconic wildlife, including koalas, kangaroos, wombats, and platypuses. The sanctuary focuses on conservation efforts and provides visitors with a hands-on, immersive experience that includes animal encounters, informative wildlife talks, and picturesque walking paths through native Australian bushland.

- Yarra Valley Chocolaterie and Ice Creamery: A must-visit for food lovers, the Yarra Valley Chocolaterie is a delightful stop for visitors seeking artisanal chocolate, handmade truffles, and decadent ice creams. Set amid beautiful gardens, the chocolatier also offers chocolate-making demonstrations and tastings, making it an enjoyable family-friendly activity.

- Scenic Drives and Lookouts: The Yarra Valley is a haven for nature lovers, with several scenic drives offering stunning views of the region's vineyards, forests, and mountain ranges. The Yarra Valley Tourist Route takes visitors through quaint towns like **Yarra Glen, Healesville, and Marysville, each offering local produce, cafes, and craft shops.

- Hot Air Ballooning: For a truly unforgettable experience, consider taking a hot air balloon ride over the Yarra Valley at sunrise. Floating above the vineyards, you'll get a bird's-eye view of the breathtaking landscape while enjoying the serenity of the valley. Many ballooning operators also offer breakfast packages at local wineries, allowing guests to indulge in delicious food while soaking in the views.

Dandenong Ranges
The Dandenong Ranges is a charming mountain range located to the east of Melbourne, offering a blend of natural beauty, lush forests, and quaint villages. Known for its cool climate, stunning gardens, and peaceful surroundings, the

Dandenongs are a great destination for a relaxing day trip, outdoor adventure, or cultural exploration.

- Puffing Billy Railway: One of the highlights of the Dandenong Ranges is the Puffing Billy Railway, a historic steam train that takes passengers on a scenic journey through the beautiful Sherbrooke Forest. This heritage railway offers a nostalgic trip through lush fern gullies and towering trees, providing a unique experience for families and train enthusiasts alike. The ride is an excellent way to immerse yourself in the natural beauty of the Dandenongs.

- National Rhododendron Gardens: The National Rhododendron Gardens is a stunning 40-hectare garden in the heart of the Dandenongs, offering a kaleidoscope of color, especially during spring when the rhododendrons bloom. The garden is home to a diverse collection of flowering plants, tranquil walking paths, and serene lakes, making it a perfect place for nature walks and photography.

- SkyHigh Mount Dandenong: For panoramic views of Melbourne and the surrounding regions, head to SkyHigh Mount Dandenong, a popular lookout point situated at the summit of Mount Dandenong. On clear days, visitors can enjoy sweeping views of the city skyline, Port Phillip Bay, and the Yarra Valley. There is also a charming café and restaurant on-site, making it a great spot for a leisurely lunch or afternoon tea.

- Olinda and Sassafras: The picturesque villages of Olinda and Sassafras are tucked away in the Dandenong Ranges, offering a charming atmosphere with boutique shops, cozy cafes, and local art galleries. Visitors can enjoy browsing handmade crafts, local produce, and beautiful antiques while strolling through the village's tree-lined streets.

- Sherbrooke Forest: A visit to Sherbrooke Forest offers a peaceful retreat into a cool temperate rainforest, where visitors can enjoy easy walking trails, birdwatching, and the chance to spot the famous Lyrebird, one of the region's most iconic species. The forest is home to giant fern trees and towering eucalyptus, providing a serene environment for nature lovers and hikers.

- William Ricketts Sanctuary: Located within the Dandenong Ranges, the William Ricketts Sanctuary is a hidden gem that showcases the works of Australian artist William Ricketts. The sanctuary features a series of clay sculptures of Aboriginal figures set within the forest, creating a deeply spiritual and reflective space that connects art, nature, and culture.

- Gardens and Parks: The Dandenong Ranges are also home to several spectacular gardens, such as Alfred Nicholas Memorial Gardens and Tesselaar Tulip Festival (held annually in spring). These gardens are perfect for a relaxing day spent among vibrant flowers and lush greenery.

Combination of Both Regions
For visitors looking to explore both regions in one trip, the Yarra Valley and Dandenong Ranges can be easily combined into a scenic loop. From wineries and wildlife experiences in the Yarra Valley to the mountain adventures and gardens of the Dandenongs, these two regions offer a diverse range of experiences that showcase the best of Victoria's natural beauty. Whether you're a wine connoisseur, nature lover, or adventure seeker, the Yarra Valley and Dandenong Ranges are must-see destinations in Victoria.

CONCLUSION

Making The Most Of Victoria

Victoria, with its diverse landscapes, vibrant cities, rich history, and incredible natural beauty, offers something for every kind of traveler. Whether you're an adventure seeker, a foodie, a culture enthusiast, or simply in search of relaxation, Victoria provides endless opportunities to explore, discover, and experience. From the bustling streets of Melbourne to the serene beauty of the Great Ocean Road, from the wine regions of the Yarra Valley to the wildlife encounters on Phillip Island, this state is full of remarkable destinations and experiences.

Making the most of your time in Victoria means embracing its natural wonders, delving into its cultural offerings, and savoring the flavors of its food and drink scene. The state's well-connected transport system makes it easy to explore both urban hotspots and remote landscapes, allowing you to experience the best of both worlds. With proper planning, budgeting, and a sense of adventure, you can craft the perfect itinerary that aligns with your interests and ensures that you experience the essence of what makes Victoria so special.

As you embark on your journey through this diverse and exciting destination, remember that the beauty of Victoria lies not just in its famous landmarks, but in the hidden gems and local experiences that truly capture its spirit. Take the time to immerse yourself in the culture, interact with the locals, and explore the many wonders that await around every corner. Whether you're visiting for a short stay or an extended adventure, Victoria promises to leave you with lasting memories and a deep appreciation for all that it has to offer.

Final Tips For An Unforgettable Trip

As you prepare for your trip to Victoria, a little planning and some insider knowledge can go a long way in ensuring your visit is both enjoyable and memorable. From exploring iconic landmarks to discovering hidden gems, here are some final tips to make your adventure in Victoria truly unforgettable:

1. Plan Ahead, but Stay Flexible: While having an itinerary is important, leave room for spontaneity. Some of the best experiences can come from unplanned moments, whether it's discovering a quiet café in a hidden laneway or stumbling upon a breathtaking view during a scenic drive.

2. Embrace Local Culture: Take the time to learn about Victoria's local traditions, history, and culture. Whether you're visiting art galleries, attending festivals, or interacting with locals, diving into the region's cultural heritage will enrich your experience and provide a deeper connection to the places you visit.

3. Pack for All Seasons: Victoria's weather can be unpredictable, so be prepared for various conditions. A light jacket, sunscreen, and layers are essential. Comfortable walking shoes are a must for exploring cities, vineyards, and national parks.

4. Use Local Transport: Victoria has a well-connected public transport system, but renting a car or hiring a bike can provide greater flexibility, especially if you're planning to explore rural areas or take scenic drives. Be sure to check local

transport schedules and road conditions before setting out.

5. Respect Nature and Wildlife: Victoria's natural beauty is one of its greatest assets, and it's crucial to preserve it for future generations. Follow Leave No Trace principles, stick to marked trails, and respect wildlife by observing from a distance. Many areas in Victoria, like Phillip Island and the Great Ocean Road, are home to endangered species, so your actions can directly impact the conservation of these remarkable habitats.

6. Taste Your Way Through the Region: Victoria is a food lover's paradise. Be sure to try local produce, wines, and dishes unique to the region. From world-class wineries in the Yarra Valley to fresh seafood along the coast, every meal offers a chance to explore the state's flavors and culinary diversity.

7. Capture the Moments: Whether it's snapping photos of stunning landscapes, recording videos of wildlife encounters, or simply enjoying the moment, make sure to capture your trip in a way that will bring you back to Victoria whenever you look through your memories.

8. Be Mindful of Time: While it's tempting to see as much as possible, don't rush your trip. Take time

to relax, enjoy the small moments, and appreciate the beauty that surrounds you. Victoria's charm lies in its details, from the tranquility of its gardens to the quiet beauty of its towns.

9. **Stay Safe and Healthy**: Make sure to follow local health guidelines, especially during busy travel periods. Carry a first aid kit, stay hydrated, and practice road safety when exploring by car. Also, make sure to have appropriate travel insurance for peace of mind during your adventures.

By following these tips, you'll not only make the most of your time in Victoria but also ensure a journey filled with unforgettable memories, experiences, and stories to share. This diverse state offers endless opportunities to connect with nature, culture, and people, making it a destination you'll want to revisit time and time again. So get ready, your unforgettable Victoria adventure is just around the corner!

Printed in Great Britain
by Amazon